A WORLD IN YOUR EAR

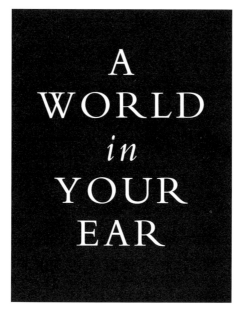

A WORLD *in* YOUR EAR

REFLECTIONS ON CHANGES

John Tusa

BROADSIDE BOOKS LIMITED

I am grateful to Malcolm Bradbury
for permission to quote from
Why Come to Slaka
(Secker & Warburg) on pages 108 to 109 in
the essay Traditore, Traduttore.

First edition published by Broadside Books Ltd 1992
2 Gurney Road, London E15 1SH
© John Tusa, 1992

Jacket design: Nigel Bradley, Publishing Projects.

Printed by: The Bath Press, Lower Bristol Road, Bath BA2 3BL

TO ALL THOSE OVER

THE LAST 60 YEARS WHO

HAVE MADE BBC WORLD SERVICE

WHAT IT IS TODAY

CONTENTS

ACKNOWLEDGEMENTS 8

INTRODUCTION 11

1
LISTENING IN CAPTIVITY 16

2
LESSONS OF THE GULF 25

3
A VERY PARTICULAR EVIL 42

4
TRUTH SAVES LIVES 56

5
VOICES IN THE DARK 69

6
BEFORE & AFTER THE FALL 85

7
TRADITORE TRADUTTORE 99

8
FOURTH ESTATE OR FIFTH COLUMN 110

9
FOURTH ESTATE OR FIRST VICTIMS 126

10
SOUND AND VISION 143

11
ANCIENT GODS & SACRED COWS 151

12
BOTTLED, CANNED OR LIVE? 163

ACKNOWLEDGEMENTS

STAN SYMINGTON of Symington Associates coined the phrase which is the title of this book while suggesting a slogan for a World Service advertisement. He generously allowed me to use it for a purpose different from the one for which it was intended. I am grateful for his imagination and his generosity.

Many of the ideas in these speeches and essays reflect the discussions about the World Service that take place between senior colleagues on a daily basis. I am grateful to them for that process and apologise if I have purloined some of their ideas without attribution.

In the last six years, we have reviewed the broadcasts and translations of all our 37 languages – Maureen Bebb has arranged or masterminded the whole process and attended almost all of the review sessions. The essay *Traditore, Traduttore* reflects that work and some of her observations. It also reflects the acute, numerous comments of our colleagues who have to render English into their own tongues.

Jim Whittell, Director of the British Council in Nigeria, invited me to Lagos to lecture to the Nigerian Institute of International Affairs. I am grateful to him and the Council for their persistence in their invitations and for their efficiency in arranging the whole trip. Michael Williams was indefatigable in devising the outlines of the lecture that I gave in Lagos.

The last six years has seen a major managerial revolution in the BBC as a whole. In considering that revolution as it affected World Service, I am grateful to John Davis, the Chief Personnel Officer, and an MBA in his own right, for keeping us and me up to the mark in terms of contemporary managerial theory. He did it with a light but effective touch.

Most of these speeches were first word-processed by my Secretary, Elizabeth Rose. She did so rapidly, efficiently and without complaint. A lot of the word-processing of the text for the book has been done by Karen McCririck. I am grateful to them both for the time it has saved me.

Throughout, my time and diary have been watched over, managed and kept within the bounds of sanity by my Personal Assistant, Diana Burnett. For what she excluded, for what she made sure found a place, and for infinite patience with sometimes endless re-arrangements, my warmest thanks.

Finally, Catherine Bradley and Broadside Books have put World Service publishing on the map in a way that many despaired of ever achieving. I hope that this Diamond Jubilee publication will reward her, as I hope it honours the organisation from which it springs.

INTRODUCTION

S IX YEARS in international broadcasting is a long time. It certainly feels it. During that time, I have visited thirty countries in connection with World Service business. I have opened relay stations or transmitter facilities in Hong Kong, Seychelles, Ascension Island and Lesotho. In the process of publicising those or other broadcasting events, I have stood in front of buffets dominated by a life size bear made out of butter in Berlin, a leaping horse (also in butter) in Beijing, a white swan (in ice) in Tokyo.

I have been criticised on local television by several Ministers of Information in Africa, publicly attacked at a mass rally by Kenya's President Daniel Arap Moi, shaken hands with the Afghan Mujahedin over the Khyber Pass, had a protest about jamming refused by the Chinese Ministry of Foreign Affairs, signed broadcasting agreements in Shanghai and Moscow, given speeches in New Orleans, New York, Tokyo, Lagos, New Delhi, Johannesburg and Cape Town, given television and radio interviews in Johannesburg, Harare, Lagos, Kuwait, Kano, Lesotho and Bahrain, argued with listeners in all those places and almost anywhere else under the sun besides. Even when listeners criticise, they do so from a standpoint of belief in the importance of what they are criticising; if it did not matter to them they would neither listen nor react.

In the last six years, I witnessed democracy breaking out in Poland, freedom and reconciliation appearing in South Africa, prudence reasserting itself in China, rehabilitation in Kuwait, transition to democracy in Nigeria, uneasy transition in Pakistan, cautious innovation in the former Soviet bloc. As political change erupted in many parts of the world, so many dictators paid the price – with their careers. There was a kind of World Service

"Curse of Gnome" on national leaders who attacked us, called for our closure, threatened our correspondents with expulsion, or otherwise tried to intimidate us or the British Government. They stood firm, as we did. Most of those who threatened us are no more. As a journalist, I shed no tears for their departure and neither did their peoples. In fact, the pinpricks of the critics were insignificant by comparison with the praise lavished on us by others.

There may be no gratitude in politics but it does seem to exist in international broadcasting. From Czechoslovakia's President Havel, to Poland's President Walesa, to former President Mikhail Gorbachev, leaders who found us a lifeline at some time or times in their lives were generous with their public praise. They cannot know how much pleasure their public acknowledgement gave to hundreds of men and women who have to believe as a matter of faith that what they broadcast in the lonely seclusion of the studio sheds light, warmth and hope in unimaginable quantities in all parts of the world. It is no diminution of their tributes to say that the words that gave most pleasure to the World Service were those of the British and American hostages released from Beirut: Terry Waite, John MacCarthy, Terry Anderson and Tom Sutherland. To listen in chains, in captivity, in solitary confinement is a metaphor in extremis of the conditions that drive many listeners to turn to the international radios. To be told that the broadcasts eased the awfulness of captivity represents the greatest reassurance about the point of the activity that anybody can imagine.

Broadcasters take a great deal on trust, even more as an act of faith. It needs only one person to testify to the value of a single broadcast to validate the whole activity. That may be too sentimental. International broadcasting requires no apology and doubts about its importance or continuing relevance usually come from people with no experience of listening at the point of need. The need is simply stated. Millions of people do not know what they need to know about the world they endure. Millions have the information kept from them. Millions live in societies where it is not available.

Almost universally, the need to know, to make sense of the world, to put it into some semblance of order, far outstrips the supply of that information, sometimes even in countries where information is theoretically both free and plentiful but technology or the structure of the market render those theoretical benefits nugatory in practice – a kind of techno-deprivation. But the justification for international broadcasting – if justification is required – is more basic.

Radio services are typically organised in horizontal strata: community radio at the most particular level of need; local radio embracing a wider community; regional radio, one stage higher in the hierarchy of communal and political awareness; national radio talking to the nation as a whole. Usually, most people stop there. In fact, international radio sits naturally at the top of that hierarchy of subject matter; it covers the world in a systematic way, whereas its national colleagues have a different agenda to address, different priorities for addressing it with, and an audience with different interests to satisfy.

International radio provides many of the services already listed; but it also provides constant, assured coverage of the world in a way that it requires, certainly deserves, and that increasing numbers of people want. If the world has become a global village, with universal sympathies and curiosity engaged by the great issues of the day, then its demanding subject matter must be treated seriously, authoritatively and with some certainty of that continuity which is essential for understanding.

International radio is therefore defined not by the ideologies of the countries to which it may speak – such as the Communist Bloc – nor by particular historical events – such as the Cold War – nor by the technology (usually short wave radio) with which it is historically associated. It is defined by the subject it deals with, by the need of those who wish to hear about it and by the fact that no other mass media vehicle meets that need in a coherent way. I have always seen the free flow of information as a basic human right, and regard the part that international broadcasting can play in delivering it as one of its most essential functions. There is no doubt that this is how the audience regards it.

In the last six years, the World Service has lost two of its languages – Japanese and Malay – and gained two – Sinhala and Ukrainian. It broadcasts for a hundred hours more each week than it did. Its audience, where it can be measured, is at least as large as it was; the Gulf Crisis demonstrated through research what we had always believed to be the case but had not been able to demonstrate – that during a crisis, listening to international radio at least doubles. To say that we are in one sense a crisis service is to define us and not to diminish us. The last six years have otherwise merely reinforced the experience and conclusions of the sixty years whose anniversary we mark in 1992. The World Service needs to speak in the international language – English – and in the main local national languages. Audiences are usually larger for the latter than for the former. Audiences are larger when we broadcast in both tongues. A constant presence is a demonstration of credibility and of good faith, an assurance that the process of communication is driven by the offer of knowledge rather than by the demands of policy. Governments who control or interfere with their international radios get the results they deserve: poor ones. The greater the operational and managerial freedom given to broadcasters, never mind the editorial freedom, the more effective the radio will be. These are simple guidelines but they have been proved to be effective. Most governments find them too difficult to put into practice; all Ministers of Information do. Listeners will put up with a bad signal; they will crowd in to a better one – audibility matters, listener loyalty is not infinite.

In the 59th year of radio, World Service at last moved into television. It was both natural to do so and essential. If the essence of the World Service is the supply of a certain class of information to certain audiences, then the only question about means of delivery relates to whether it is appropriate and to whom it gives access. Clearly, television reaches certain influential audiences who are more firmly in the television age than the radio age. To the extent that we had lost these audiences – say the affluent Indian middle class, because they had "migrated" to television – it was essential to recover them. To the extent that they had never had the habit of listening to the BBC World Service, it was necessary to win them over. In markets such as the Indian sub-continent, television strengthens us by giving us a place in a strong, affluent, influential section of the audience. Yet the needs, the numbers of those in other, less favoured, economic and political classes remain urgent, clamorous and must be satisfied in the only way possible, and the best way appropriate – by radio. In this respect, the relationship of WSTV to WS radio is akin to that between radio broadcasts in English and any other great national language – our audiences are stronger when we broadcast in both. Similarly our competitive position with other broadcasters is immensely strengthened by being able to talk to audiences in two strong mediums – radio, with its range, its spread, its flexibility, its cheapness, its unstoppability; television, with its intensity, its passion, its unforgettability. In our 60th year, the fact that our editorial voice and approach is conveyed by two media of communication represents a historic strengthening of our influence.

A final word of warning. The World Service is strong, independent, credible, effective and influential because it is a part of the BBC. We are part of an institution which takes its stand on editorial independence and impartiality, on a public service approach to the audience, which gains strength from being a large composite news-making and news-breaking organisation, which cross-fertilises through the exchange of staff at all levels. Were the BBC to be undermined, were the World Service to become part of a weaker, more vulnerable broadcasting institution, then the values of the World Service which so many have relied on for 60 years and so many others take for granted, could be gravely threatened.

CHAPTER 1
LISTENING IN CAPTIVITY

T HE LIBERATION of the British and American hostages held in Beirut has drawn attention in the most intense and public way to the power of radio. I know of nobody directly involved in the World Service – or in the BBC for that matter – who did not listen to the striking and moving testimonies of the freed men to the part played by the World Service in their survival without a sense of some emotion and near disbelief. The deeply considered testimony from Terry Waite which he gave on his return to RAF Lyneham deserves recording in full:

> The occasion today would not be complete without a word of special thanks and affection to the World Service of the BBC. For four years again one had nothing and then out of the blue a small radio appeared. Just a cheap set and I said 'Thank God I'm in the Middle East where the World Service can be received on the medium wave for virtually twenty-four hours a day.' In the last twelve months the World Service helped keep us alive both spiritually through the work of the religious department and mentally through the variety of cultural and news programmes that are broadcast with such excellence. Thank you World Service. Thank you very much.

Apart from anything else, his acknowledgement of the value of the totality of World Service radio output is significant. We have always believed in the importance of an all-purpose network rather than a more specialist all-news network. Here was one person who found that man does not live by news alone.

But it was the American Tom Sutherland's tribute to the World Service that took my own breath away. As I watched his arrival in

Damascus on the BBC Nine O'Clock News, I was not wondering if he would refer to the World Service. Yet as he opened his mouth, I knew instinctively that he would, though I could not have dared to imagine the lines that he would deliver in that intoxicated rush of excitement at being free:

> VOA [Voice of America] is an excellent radio station, but I'm afraid I have to admit that the BBC has everybody beaten hands down. I would guess that if one took a bunch of money and I don't know how much they get, but it must be a lot and said to a director put together the best kind of international radio that you could possibly devise I think you would come up with something like the BBC. So, Mr. Ambassador, my thanks. When I hear people like Barbara Myers on Outlook and John Tidmarsh on Outlook and such fantastically competent reporters as you have in Russia and India and China I will be writing to some of them to tell them about the information they gave us and kept our minds alive and working during this period of captivity.

We have always maintained that radio listening, especially to international radio, is driven by real need, that its justification lies in its capacity to reassure, support and inform a huge agglomeration of individuals scattered around the world; we have always had to take what we do with a large measure of trust, believing that it is doing what we hope it does. Every day, World Service broadcasters "fire their arrows in the air, they come to earth we know not where."

In the last four months, the compelling testimonies just quoted, not to mention those of President Gorbachev and the other Beirut hostages, John McCarthy and Terry Anderson have told us – and the world – that we have been hitting a series of bulls eyes.

While we are on the subject, it is worth putting on the record exactly what Mr. Gorbachev did and did not say on his release from detention in his Crimean dacha. On August 22, 1991 he described his brief captivity to journalists at the Soviet Foreign Ministry's Press Centre. With his telephone lines cut off, he and his family and staff did manage to find out what was going on: "Everything was cut off but we found an old radio set, readjusted the aerial so that we could receive some foreign programmes and then we got the BBC best of all. The BBC best of all."

It has been objected that all Gorbachev actually said was that he had "received" the BBC best of all – that this was a reception report and not a comment on the quality or excellence of the programmes of the BBC Russian Service. Yet it was clear from the laughter and applause from the international press that greeted his remarks that they all took it as I believe it was meant – as a tribute both to the BBC Russian Service's journalism, as well as their audibility. After all, at the same news conference, Gorbachev asked where the BBC correspondent was and when it turned out he was not present – they were probably monitoring it on tv in the BBC office – Gorbachev said: "Never mind. The BBC knows everything already."

Any doubts there might still be on the sense of his remarks were removed the following day when Gorbachev went to the Russian Parliament to thank them for their steadfastness and to thank Yeltsin for rescuing him: "I listened to the BBC and picked up some information for the first time after my bodyguards managed to find some wire and fix some old receivers. We picked up the reports of a correspondent who, it transpires, was actually here in this building, inside it."

This process of direct communication with individual listeners has been going on since the dawn of international radio. On September 25th, 1991, we celebrated the life and broadcasts of one of Bush House's most influential commentators, Maurice Latey. It included this tribute from Leonid Finkelstein of the BBC Russian Service, who met Latey only in 1966 but felt that he had known him as a personal friend for almost 20 years before that. How could Finkelstein have come to believe that?

In 1947, like millions of my compatriots, I was arrested and sent to Gulag prison camps. In one of them where I remained for several years, there was a skilful electrician named Fedorchenko. In his tiny workshop full of junk, amidst bundles of wire, discarded fittings, bulbs, old valves and the like there existed a cleverly hidden receiver. He would invite me there, give me a single headphone – and there was Maurice talking!

Maurice Latey was not talking to Leonid Finkelstein personally; but Finkelstein felt that he was. That is why we listen to radio. In captivity, needs must where the devil drives, and fortunately prison guards are often idle, stupid and venal – as well as violent and brutal. Or just plain unobservant. The BBC Polish Service tells the story of the Darlowek internment camp where most of the Polish intellectual and political elite were imprisoned after the imposition of martial law in 1981. Now a senior member of the Polish parliament, Alexander Malachowski used to listen to the radio by hiding it under his long bushy beard while others took compulsory exercise. He would then brief his friends about what had been broadcast when they returned. I do not know what the Polish word for "ben trovato" is but I rather think it may apply to that story. It is a fact, however, that Malachowski thanked the Polish Section publicly in 1990 for the service they provided during martial law.

The radio sustained Lech Walesa during his imprisonment, when his political career looked to most people as if it was at an end. In his autobiography, *A Path of Hope*, Walesa includes this account by his wife Danuta of her visits to him in jail:

I was surprised to find that Lech had a shortwave radio on which he could listen to the Polish language broadcasts from the West. He was constantly listening to Radio Free Europe the Voice of America, the BBC, whatever he could get, and he drove the guards so crazy that after a while they announced that the radio was broken. I can understand how they felt, because I know how loud he plays the radio. It makes such a racket your head feels as if it's about to explode. One of the guards complained that it gave him migraines. Lech sat at the radio all day long, fiddling with the knob.

But what exactly does the service amount to? Living as we do in an environment saturated with information, it is next to impossible to comprehend its impact in a world where it is controlled. Fortunately, occasional letter-writers capture this impact with a vivid intensity that stops you short. From Sofia, in Bulgaria, this letter reached us earlier this year:

> *I am your listener since 1943, when the authorities sealed our new Telefunken with red wax, to prevent us from hearing the voice of truth. Although the youngest in the family, I was the first to break the seal.*

This year, too, there was a letter from Romania, from a listener who spoke of being subjected to the "moral terror" of the Ceausescu regime:

> *I used to listen to your broadcasts with the volume turned down as far as possible so as not to be heard by my neighbours through the thin walls of the building. But your news reached me. It gave me strength, it healed me, it gave me hope for a freer future. Your news gave one confidence, made one feel a human being, not a slave.*

After the anti-Gorbachev coup we received many letters from the Soviet Union showing that Mikhail Sergeyevich himself had not been the only person who relied on the BBC as an essential means of information. One wrote from Ulyanovsk region (to the east of Moscow), describing how the listener had struggled to establish the facts of what was going on:

> *In one room, I was able to hear an announcer of the Soviet TV reading out new decrees proclaimed by Yenaev's gang, in another room the BBC Russian Service was giving us complete up-to-date information of happenings in Moscow and the rest of the country. It was that conjunction of incoming information that made me quickly realise that the gang of eight won't stay long. It wasn't that you were giving us the answer. But your response to the events, your analytical talks, helped me to form my own opinion.*

If radio has that sort of power of communicating to the single person, its effect when it focusses directly on the plight of a particular individual can be even more dramatic. Terry Waite, John McCarthy and Tom Sutherland have all spoken with affection of the special support that they received from the *Outlook* team of John Tidmarsh, Barbara Myers and John Waite. Their achievement was to talk to one person without excluding the rest of the audience. Who could not have been moved by the sound of John and David Waite talking to Terry while he was still in chains, and playing his favourite pieces of Bach? There was no question of eavesdropping on a private telephone call. It was a direct communication to a particular person which carried with it the appeal of universality. In speaking to Terry or John or the others, they were speaking to all detainees. I take this opportunity of acknowledging the *Outlook* team's professionalism, sensitivity and humanity. The same should be said of the Gulf Link team who spoke even more directly to the Britons detained by Saddam Hussein until December 12th, 1990. The team received a Christmas card the other day from a former detainee: "Terry Waite got it right – you kept us alive."

For some, that phrase is more than understandable and forgiveable hyperbole. A young Tamil emerged from the Boosa detention camp in Sri Lanka shattered by the experience. He wrote to us, the first letter he had written, he said, in 18 months:

> *Although the local Sri Lanka radio tried to brainwash us, we were careful. But we were able to listen to the BBC at night. The BBC Tamil Service was my consolation. I would translate Tamilosai news to my Sinhala friends. We learnt about the good work done by the Amnesty International and the Women's Front in Sri Lanka through the BBC. There were days when I would feel like committing suicide after a day's torture. But the BBC and Shankar Anna would be there in the evening to reassure me and keep me sane. Please continue with your good work. Be with my Sinhala and Tamil friends I left behind in the Boosa Detention Camp. Please reach them and console them. Keep them sane!*

21

(It is worth reflecting that the Tamil Service consists of just three members of staff and costs only £224,000 per year to run.)

And the stories go on and on – from every continent. Amnesty International has a great deal of evidence that its letter–writing campaigns in support of prisoners of conscience do have an effect on the way they are treated. Being mentioned on the radio appears to have a similar effect. In Malawi, the distinguished poet, Jack Mapanje, recently emerged from three years' detention. He knew he had not been forgotten because a friendly gaoler told him each time he was mentioned on the BBC African Service.

In Hungary, the noted left-wing writer George Paloczi-Horvath, was in gaol. One day a young secret police lieutenant came into the cell carrying sausages and other luxuries. Asked why he had singled out Paloczi-Horvath for this attention, the secret police-man replied: "Sir, my family are from your estates." Asked how he learned where the feudal land was, he replied it was from listening to the BBC Hungarian Service.

There are moments of humour in these letters, even when listening in captivity. In August 1990, we received a cheerful letter from a detained Briton in Baghdad. He was anxious that lengthy detention would make him lose touch with Dave Lee Travis's *Jolly Good Show* on the *BBC Wild Service*. Fortunately, they were given a radio so they asked DLT for a request:

> The nine of us here would like to dedicate a record to the President of Iraq and the National Assembly. It should not surprise you if we request 'Please Release Me', sung by E. Humperdinck.

Another lighter occasion comes from the BBC Turkish Service, who treasure this tale from the jails from the years 1980/81:

> The ultra right wing (MHP) and Islamic fundamentalist (MPS) plus party officials are in the same ward in a Turkish military prison. The right-wingers are avid listeners to the BBC Turkish output. Islamics spend their time praying. One Islamic is reputedly very good in interpreting the dreams. So a prominent right-wing

MP corners him one morning and says in his dream he saw all the headlines and the news in the day's papers. When the papers arrive he is right to a comma. This happens every day. The right-winger is elevated to prophet status by all. That is until someone realises that the BBC output at 22.45 Turkish time carries a review of next day's Turkish papers!

We must not forget those still detained and who may or may not be listening in captivity: Aung San Suu Kyi, the Nobel Peace Prize winner, and leader of the Burmese Democracy movement, detained under house arrest by the Burmese military since July 1989. We know that she listened in the early part of her detention. Ne Min, a Burmese lawyer who was sentenced by the military regime to fourteen years' hard labour for allegedly "knowingly passing on false news", appears to be one of those cases where publicity provokes even worse treatment from his captors. That is a measure of the nature of the present Burmese government. Let us hope that those in detention are still listening, for as Andrei Sakharov wrote about his own exile in Gorky, "a person deprived of connection to the outside world becomes a living corpse." It would be wonderful if Amnesty International started a fund to supply a radio to those in prison. Of course, many regimes would reject them out of hand; some would not. Even if it prevented one detainee from becoming a "living corpse", what an achievement that would be.

Imprisonment may be spiritual as well as physical but just as bad for that. The late Dr. Roberto Arias, husband of the great British dancer Dame Margot Fonteyn, was a quadraplegic for the last decade of his life. His mind remained perfectly alert. With a specially adapted gadget he could tune his radio to hear the programmes that he wanted: it sustained him while he was – as he told a friend – "a captive in my own body."

Sometimes the list of those who have stated publicly how essential World Service broadcasts were to them in their captivity reads like a modern *Who's Who*. Benazir Bhutto and Asghar Khan from Pakistan, Begum Khalida Zia from Bangladesh, George Fernandes from India, Bulent Ecevit and Suleyman Demirel from

Turkey, Lech Walesa from Poland – these names are just a few of those on this roll of honour. Their significance is not that they were or are important politically. The World Service talks to the strong and the weak, the powerful and the helpless, the known and the obscure. That is our strength. Whoever they are, we talk to them, and they listen to us, as individuals. If I should have to choose between the categories and could only broadcast to one of them, I know what my choice would be. Fortunately, since we broadcast rather than narrowcast, we do not have to make the choice.

The experience of listening in captivity was eloquently summed up by Paul Donovan in the *Sunday Times* on November 24th 1991. He wrote:

> *The next time someone puts forward the notion that radio no longer matters in the age of television, let them remember that it is radio that helped to keep good men sane in the hour when they needed it most.*

Radio – international or domestic – is at once an act of public and private communication; it manages to be both general to its audience and particular to each member of it; it can sway millions, but it does so through millions of individual moments of listening; it is a gesture of human outreach which can go straight to the heart. And as our letter-writers have told us, it healed them, it kept them sane, it helped them to form their own opinion, it broke the seal of ignorance and lies. Radio is the least coercive of media; it respects the listeners too much. That is why we are lucky to work in it, are proud of doing so, and why today we give special recognition to those who have demonstrated how compassionate and humane it can be.

First given as a speech to the Radio Academy on 10 December 1991.

CHAPTER 2

THE LESSONS
OF THE GULF WAR

IT WAS clear during the suppression of the Tiananmen Square Democracy movement in June 1989; it was confirmed during the Revolution in Eastern Europe in Autumn 1989; it was validated by the Gulf War of 1990-91 – when the international scene convulses, the leaders and the led, the victors and the victims, the players and the watchers in the mass audience turned to one news source above others for their picture of events – the BBC's World Service. It was a remarkable tribute to a British institution, that the news from London, even during a crisis where Britain was deeply involved, was regarded as the one to turn to, certainly to monitor, and for many, to trust.

The Gulf War was a landmark in the broadcasting history of the World Service in various ways. It demonstrated the wisdom of an observation made by a great wartime figure, Sir Robert Bruce Lockhart, Head of the Political Warfare Executive. Writing from retirement in 1959, Lockhart stated: "Broadcasting in the External Services cannot be turned on and off like a water tap... Broadcasting services have to be kept in a state of readiness". In similar vein, the former Director General of the BBC and one time director of Overseas Services, Sir Ian Jacob, wrote in 1957; "To seek to save the cost of a particular language on the grounds that problems are unlikely to arise in that particular area is like an attempt to pick out the notes of a piano keyboard that will not be wanted".

Both observations remain true today. The World Service can only be effective in a crisis if it has been broadcasting regularly to the area concerned for years past. That is the basis on which trust is forged with the audience, reliability established and credibility confirmed. Effectiveness springs from being able to broadcast to masses of listeners in the local national language or languages. The World Service would not have had the impact that it had, unless it had been able to speak to the Chinese in Mandarin, the Poles in Polish or the Arab World in Arabic during the extraordinary world events of 1989-1990.

The experience of broadcasting during the Gulf War is worth examining. After the Suez Crisis of 1956 and the fall of the Shah of Iran in 1978, it set the World Service as a whole, and the BBC Arabic Service in particular, one of the most severe editorial challenges of their existence. As the Gulf Crisis developed, there was one over-riding concern in our minds: to manage and supervise the editorial output so securely that nobody would be able to prove the charge that either the language broadcasts were deviating from BBC editorial standards, or that we were doing anything other than providing consistent, balanced and unbiased coverage. We accepted that no one could be prevented from levelling such charges but were resigned to the fact that, once made, they would have to be answered seriously, accurately and utterly convincingly.

It was with that sense of foreboding and realism that we faced the early days of the crisis which began on August 2, 1990 when Iraqi forces invaded Kuwait. The World Service's response was complex, consumed large quantities of management time, and required considerable internal coordination. I will take it in five sections: how we changed the broadcasts to meet the demand of events; how many people listened to those broadcasts; how the listeners reacted; how the World Service responded to external criticism of the broadcasts; and finally, what conclusions we drew at the end about our journalistic response.

From the moment that the Iraqi invasion occurred, it was evident that a swift broadcasting response was needed. Whatever might happen subsequently, the invasion altered the world. Within hours of the invasion on August 2, 1990 we increased (with Foreign Office approval) the broadcasts of the Arabic Service from the existing nine hours to ten and a half. Later they were extended still further to fourteen hours a day. Within 24 hours of the Iraqi attack, jamming of the Arabic Service was observed. It was of the characteristic "wobble type" modulation used by Iraq when it had jammed the BBC and other western broadcasters during the Iran-Iraq war, as soon as US news correspondents broadcast reports of Iraq's use of chemical weapons. The jamming site was tentatively located as being close to Baghdad, to the south-east of the city. By August 8, it was decided to swamp the jamming by increasing the numbers of frequencies used by the BBC Arabic Service. Accordingly, World Service planners and engineers deployed spare transmitter and frequency time to virtually double the Arabic signal – expanding from four to seven frequencies in the morning, and from six to eleven in the peak evening listening time. The tactic was successful. The higher frequencies were particularly difficult to jam and after some nine weeks, the jamming stopped altogether, possibly because of the cost of the electricity needed to power it.

The immediate response went beyond the Arabic Service. Many listeners to the World Service in English lived or worked in the Gulf and Middle East. Usually, World Service does not target its programmes to that area in the night hours because the audience is asleep and it would be a huge waste of electricity. In such crisis conditions, it was felt wrong to deny listeners access to news programmes at any time of day or night. World Service (English) on both Short and Medium Wave was put onto a 24 hour trans-mission pattern to the Middle East from the night of August 8th - 9th.

But listening to Iraq was almost as vital as broadcasting to the area. At BBC Monitoring at Caversham Park, near Reading, where international broadcasts are monitored for news and official statements, two extra staff were allocated to cover broadcasts from the Gulf. Further monitoring effort was directed at Iraq to make sure that none of Saddam Hussein's statements would be overlooked.

The reaction to these moves was immediate and gratifying. A World Service listener from Madina in Saudi Arabia wrote to the

Arabic Service in early August:

> *The extension of your transmissions, for both periods, was a positive step which increased the confidence of the Arab listener in you. I personally have seen the ordinary listener, the man in the street, hurrying to buy a radio set and insisting that it should be able to receive 'London Radio'. From my observations, the people are extremely interested in your broadcast and are not bothering with anyone else's.*

At about the same time a British technician wrote to the World Service newsroom from Saudi Arabia thanking them for the accuracy of the coverage of events in the area. He added:

> *Regarding the World Service News – in English – please keep up the good work. Each hour sees all the many nationalities in here crowded around the now rarely available short wave radio sets.*

But at a time of such crisis, we were aware that we must use our airwaves to talk very directly to the tens of thousands of third party nationals marooned, threatened, jobless, or as in the case of Americans and British citizens in Iraq, detained against their will by Saddam Hussein. For the latter, we devised "Gulf Link" a programme of special and personal messages from family and friends to their relatives held hostage in Iraq or Kuwait. Starting at fifteen minutes a day, it rapidly grew to half an hour per day, transmitted on one special frequency at 1645 hours GMT, expanding to forty-five minutes on three frequencies. It forged a strong bond between the divided families and was often intensely moving to listen to. Those in Britain soon got into the habit of regularly delivering their messages on tape for broadcast; the hostages themselves grew devoted to the presenters of the programme and were overwhelming in their gratitude to them when they were freed in early December.

The plight of the tens of thousands of migrant workers in the Gulf from Asian nationalities was also not ignored. Existing broadcasts in Hindi, Urdu, Pashto and Persian were easily heard in the Gulf area as a matter of course. Knowing of the beleaguered existence of thousands of Thais, Bengalis and Indonesians in the Gulf, we allocated each of these 3 services an extra frequency so that they too could be heard by their nationals stuck in the turmoil of the crisis. This action not only earned the gratitude of the governments concerned, but that of the listeners too.

The Thai Chargé d'Affaires in London phoned the Thai Service to say that he had been instructed by his government to convey "heartfelt thanks" for the special broadcasts. The Thai Airways Manager based in Dahran, Saudi Arabia reported they were of enormous importance and benefit. He reported too, the case of a group of Thais attempting to flee from occupied Kuwait, and losing heart in the middle of the desert when they doubted if they would be permitted entry by the Saudi authorities. They tuned to a BBC Thai transmission, heard of other Thais who had crossed near Al Khafji successfully, and pressed on to safety on the strength of that information. Letters from Bengalis in Qatar confirmed the importance of the added frequency, such as the one that wrote: "It is the BBC alone which has provided us with detailed and analytical news".

It was essential as a world broadcaster to demonstrate that concern for distressed citizens did not stop at the shores of Great Britain, but included those nationals whom we were in a position to help at minimal extra cost. At such times, the question of nationality is secondary to the humanitarian instinct of helping all listeners in need; such a response is fundamental to international broadcasting. This tribute was only one of many:

> *Words can't really explain what it's been like. The BBC World Service has been our only link with the outside world. Everyone knows the signature tune to that programme extremely well now and every single word is dissected until the next hour's bulletin.*

It happened to come from a British woman who escaped from

Kuwait at the end of August, but its messsage was almost universal.

The messages came not in individual bursts – the mail came in shoals. We analysed the 23,000 letters which reached our Audience Research department on the crisis in general. I will exclude a curious distorting factor – 15,763 letters came from Tamil Nadu, most of them complimentary. I don't mean to disparage our Tamil listeners, but a more balanced global picture emerges if we look at the remaining 7,205 letters. Many wrote about the event and not about our coverage. Of those which referred directly to our coverage, 75% were complimentary. This was not the case evenly throughout the world. Of the 777 letters in Hausa, 650 were critical of our coverage. I remind you that in December 1990, listeners to the Hausa Service named Saddam Hussein as the Man of the Year. A thousand letters came to the Somali Service, and 60% of them were pro-Saddam. Of the 107 letters received by World Service in English, 80 were critical, some objecting to the changes in the schedule, others accusing us of bias towards Saddam Hussein. Elsewhere the post bag in Hindi, Urdu, Bengali, Indonesian, Turkish and Chinese was overwhelmingly positive about our coverage.

Yet anecdotes and thousands of letters remain only that; individual reactions are only valid in their own broad opinion. It was essential to acquire measured assessment of the audience size and its behaviour. The received wisdom in the World Service has always been that listening increases sharply during a crisis. Common sense as well as circumstantial evidence have always pointed in that direction. Yet it remained only an educated guess, not yet backed with statistical evidence. During the Gulf crisis we were in a position to test the assumption, and while the crisis affected a wide geographical area, many parts of it were open to research. That research was conducted in various different states and at different stages of the crisis. The results were revealing and remarkably consistent.

We have three pieces of market research to give us an idea of the extent of listening, conducted at three distinct periods of the crisis.

By the end of August 1990, we had completed a survey in the United Arab Emirates, Riyadh, and Cairo and Alexandria. The figures for Cairo and Alexandria were typical of those for the entire survey. Before the crisis, 18% of the audience listened to BBC World Service at least once a week. After the crisis, the figure rose almost three-fold to 46%. In addition, 28% said they had listened "yesterday", confirming the picture of serious and regular listening. The BBC emerged as the most listened-to foreign broadcaster, ahead of Saudi Radio and the commercial Radio Monte Carlo.

How important was the BBC as a news source at the start of the crisis? 6% of the sample in Cairo and Alexandria said they first heard of the invasion of Kuwait from the BBC World Service. But 37% tuned to us for confirmation of the event and/or for further information. Those who mentioned radio in general as a source for news in Cairo and Alexandria were 75%, against 74% who mentioned television, and 25% who said they turned to newsprint.

In Cairo and Alexandria, 91% of our audience listened in Arabic, the remaining 9% in English. The pattern in Riyadh and the Emirates was very similar – a large leap in listening to us as the crisis began; and subsequent heavy use of the BBC as a confirmatory source or one for further information.

Four months into the crisis, in November, further research was conducted in the Jordanian capital, Amman. It showed that our weekly audience was 43% of the total. This gave us a listenership twice as large as Radio Monte Carlo, and four times as large as the Voice of America. 82% of the audience cited radio as their principal source of news, while 73% mentioned TV. Once people first heard of the crisis, 28% said they turned to the BBC World Service for more news about it.

Further research was conducted in Amman in May 1991, two months after the Gulf war had left the headlines. While the "crisis" listening figures to the BBC had fallen to a regular audience of 27%, this still left the Arabic Service well ahead of its international competitors – mainly around 10% – and just ahead of its populist competitor, Radio Monte Carlo. This further research therefore established two facts: first the strong position of the Arabic Service under "normal" circumstances, and, second, its even greater strength during a crisis even among listeners in a country which often disapproved of the news they felt they were getting from the BBC.

The final piece in this intensive survey of crisis listening in the Middle East came from Syria in February 1991. At 15.6% of the audience in Damascus and Aleppo, the BBC was the second largest foreign broadcaster, second only to Radio Monte Carlo. The daily audience was four times as large as that for the Voice of America. But among BBC listeners, the patterns of tuning in were intensive – 79% of the BBC's audience said they had tuned in the day before they were interviewed, an unusually high figure.

Finally, there was a qualitative indicator. In the Amman research, as well as that in the Syrian cities, the listeners were asked to score BBC news coverage on a scale from zero to 5. In Amman, we scored 3.25, but in Damascus and Aleppo the figure was notably higher at 4.07.

The conclusions from this most detailed set of surveys of listening during a crisis were encouraging. First, they confirmed that the audience did indeed grow dramatically at such times of acute information need. It also grew for reasons consistent with the World Service's aims and purposes. Listeners expected reliability, constancy and authority and voted for us favourably with their radio set tuning knobs. Secondly, it reminded those who think of television as the only mass medium, that when it comes to international news, radio plays as large a part in informing the public as does television. Thirdly, more parochially for us, it spoke well of our standing *vis-a-vis* our main rivals and competitors. Fourthly, it raised searching questions about the correct way of measuring the audience for international broadcasting. The standard definition of "a listener" is a person who listens "regularly at least once a week". Yet if international radio is distinctively a communicator at times of need, those who find it essential, indeed life-saving at such times, must surely count as part of the audience just as much as those who happen to listen regularly. If the broadcasts are to be effective when the need arises – almost always suddenly and without warning – then that is a powerful message to the broadcasters; they must be present even when they may not always be much listened to. But the message to researchers is that the yardstick of measurement must include those who use the service only occasionally. The listener in a crisis is as much a valued and significant listener as the regular patron. So far, audience measurements have not adapted to take account of this new perception.

But the audience's individual reaction did matter and although it is impossible to draw statistical conclusions from them, letters carry a message, especially when they arrive in such numbers, and often so passionately argued. It seemed as if many listeners were using the radio like a close friend, with whom they would argue intensely – and were upset when a difference of views arose.

But the generally reassuring and supporting message from the audience research and the listeners' correspondence did not end the matter. With so much at stake for governments as well as people, it was only to be expected that governments would listen closely, and that they would have a view about what they heard. Some Arab governments did not like what they heard and complained to the British government and to the BBC about it. The only correct and prudent response was to demonstrate that the criticisms were being taken seriously, that they would be investigated, that changes would be made if any criticisms proved accurate or well founded, and that detailed monitoring of Arabic Service output was being undertaken.

But just as editorial independence is the BBC's responsibility, so is the responsibility to implement it. Normal monitoring of output is a routine part of editorial activity. Additional editorial monitoring was instituted in several additional ways and at different levels. The Arabic Service had a sound historical reputation for accuracy and impartiality, and its senior management were all - regardless – of nationality – long imbued with BBC editorial values. Now they were to be more rigorously scrutinised than any language service other than English had ever been.

First of all, retrospective analysis was carried out. We made weekly tallies of current affairs items, analysed by subject matter, dateline, origin and nationality of speaker. Over several weeks this review demonstrated that we had not – as was alleged – given more reports from Baghdad than from the alliance countries, or that there were more Iraqi spokesmen heard in voice than those from the alliance. During these reviews, we did point out to our critics that if the news had been covered by more western journalists working from Iraq, the tallies might, rightly, have shown a different result. We also pointed out to Saudis and Gulfis that if their Ministers were heard less frequently on the air than Saddam Hussein, Tariq Aziz, Latif Jassim, Dr. Al Anbari or whoever, then this reflected Saudi reluctance to give interviews.

Secondly, we checked the running orders of all the Arabic Service current affairs programmes for any possible distortion of emphasis. Thirdly, I felt that I needed some more personal reassurance that the Arabic Service was doing what we believed it was – broadcasting fairly according to BBC editorial standards. After consultation, I was recommended a distinguished Arab living in London, with a long, impeccable record in academic and business life. He agreed to listen to some five hours of Arabic Service output on a weekly basis. Recordings of selected transmissions were made without the knowledge of the Service. The "listener" was sent the cassettes on a Friday afternoon. We spoke on the following Monday when he would give me a detailed response to the editorial style, content, tone, approach of the programmes. Nobody but myself – or on two occasions my Deputy – was involved in these conversations.

As a result, I could say with some confidence that the accusations of inaccurate translations, bias in coverage, or a sneering tone of delivery levelled against the Arabic Service, were not justified. By chance, one of the days selected for recording was that when the allied bomb hit the Baghdad shelter, killing women and children. On that day, many of the members of the Arabic Service were deeply troubled and upset by the killings. My "listener" told me that he could detect nothing in their voices, intonations, inflections or language that even hinted at the turmoil they felt.

Over time the complaints died away. The thoroughness of the scrutiny and its total failure to confirm the accuracy of the complaints slowly won over all but the most outspoken of the doubters. The determination to carry it out was quite as important as what it revealed. Emotions, too, in the region itself died down. So why had the complainants been so passionate in their beliefs? There is no single explanation, and different individuals would give different reasons for objecting. But they are almost certainly a composite of the following ingredients: first, many listeners did not like hearing what they did – either news that Saddam Hussein was losing, or news that Saddam Hussein was saying anything and was being reported; secondly, some listeners were hearing things that they knew they would never hear on their own media and disliked it on that account or were shocked by what they heard; thirdly, some listeners wanted the BBC to be on their side, whatever side that was, and were disappointed when we were not; fourthly, some listeners reacted adversely to the nationalities of certain broadcasters on the Arabic Service, assuming that a Palestinian or Jordanian had to be pro-Saddam because of the policies of their respective national leaders; fifthly, some supporters of Saddam Hussein assumed that the BBC was institutionally anti-Saddam because it was reporting news from the allied headquarters, while others assumed that we were pro-Saddam because we reported from Baghdad. Faced with such a tally of conflicting and irreconcilable demands, it was possible only to monitor vigilantly, and take refuge in the solid evidence of the research and even of the correspondence, both of which revealed a solid, majority bedrock of support, approval and trust.

When it was all over, the self-criticism began. At a Bush House internal seminar on April 11, 1991, the overall conclusion was that the coverage had been extensive, wide-ranging, detailed, and reasonably balanced. There were many technical anxieties about the way in which information was collected, processed and distributed within the World Service, about the balance between speculation and analysis, the reliance on official news sources and much else besides. But it was against a background of feeling that the job had been reasonably accomplished that I went to the Public Radio Conference in America in May 1991 and listened to their debate on the coverage of the Gulf War. This was the mood that I noted in my diary of the time:

> What emerges from the session is a strong current of hostility to coverage of the war, an overt belief that the Pentagon "lied" to the press and that the press were too dumb or too docile to notice; strong feelings that the war was covered in a "hurray" manner, that objectivity went out of the window, and that the slight complacency felt about the coverage was thoroughly undeserved. When the questions began, the general assumption was that the government had not even dressed up its information under the guise of military exigency but was merely untrustworthy. The shadow of Vietnam, the Pentagon Papers, Nixon and Watergate, the Iran-Contra affair – the long list of governmental duplicity in the presentation and control of news.

But that debate, scrappy, bad-tempered, needlessly self-flagellating as I thought it was, forced me to crystallise my own thoughts on the war and our broadcasts, coverage which had stood examination from the listeners and won plaudits from them. Yet nothing is ever so simple, and even when the verdict is essentially positive there are many ways in which it can be improved in the future. Written during the PRC conference in May 1991, these comments still reflect my considered thoughts on the subject:

> First, there were a lot of aspects that were missed and under-reported – though seldom in my view the questions about which the complaints are regularly made. Biggest miss was the full realisation of the meaning of Bush's doubling of the ground troops in October. Yes, it was covered – how could it not be? Yet its full implication,

that war was inevitable, was given insufficient weight. Did we sufficiently appreciate how the US military had changed its thinking in the aftermath of Vietnam? Or how sophisticated they had become militarily? Secondly, the West treated Saddam Hussein as a political leader working within the recognisable conventions of international politics. He would huff and puff and then withdraw at the last moment because that was what rational leaders would do. The fact that he could emerge strengthened from a late, daring tactical withdrawal made it an obvious Machiavellian manoeuvre. Only John Simpson spotted that he was different, a street brawler who did not play by the Queensberry rules of international politics, a fighter who not only threw his opponent out of the ring, but descended into the audience and started head-butting them for good measure. The critics of coverage who complain Hussein was treated and tarred – somehow unreasonably – as a villain, totally miss the point. He is far more wicked than even Bush said or perhaps can even imagine. His capacity for constant destruction and killing to stay in power is breathtaking – as we said of the US firepower deployed against him, "awesome" – and still underestimated. Most people will do a lot to hang on to power – it is genuinely hard to handle somebody who will do anything to stay in power.

Thirdly, we did not adequately tell our listeners/readers what they were NOT being told. It was right to report the official version of events but we should have reminded them more often that large areas of activity were being under-reported or not reported at all because there was no information about them.

Fourthly, we did not tell them the obvious – you cannot bomb a country and its forces so heavily and for so long without its making a difference. I do not agree with the John Keegan view that tv presenters were knaves and fools for not saying simply and clearly that it was going to be a walk over from the beginning. I do think we could have reported both that no battle can be taken for granted, and that such a weight of bombing could point only in one direction and to one conclusion. Finally, I think that from time to time we took the "Arabists" and the environmentalists too seriously. The scaremongers in both camps said variously that the Arab world would rise up in response to Saddam's call; that terrorism would break out in a fifth column of pro-Saddamism; that the Arab moderates would be overthrown for supporting the Coalition; that the Persian Gulf would be polluted for a generation by the oil pumping by Saddam; that the weather would be changed by the oil well fires; that the casualties would be counted in tens of thousands; that the sight of body bags on the lines of a WWI cemetery would appal the US public and panic them into a Vietnam- style retreat. Und so weiter, und so weiter.

Well, we reported it in the interests of fairness – but did we test, probe and question these nightmare scenarios adequately? Come to that, did we test the Iraqui spokesmen, the Ambassadors, the Information Minister adequately? I think not. Too often they were allowed to make uncontested assertions of a very debatable kind. Bob Jobbins (Editor of World Service News) believes that in the interests of balance and fair reporting we allowed too many wholly incredible statements from Baghdad onto the air. We had to report even-handedly, but there must be a better way of addressing this problem.

Where are we? We were inconsistent in first pillorying Bush for the Mutla Ridge slaughter, the pressure on the so-called "hidden agenda" to take Baghdad, and then when Schwarzkopf stayed his hand – or Bush stayed it for him – and Saddam turned on the Shia and the Kurds, we blamed Bush. We let Schwarzkopf off very lightly for saying he had been "suckered" over the helicopter agreement. This was no grounds for sitting back and letting Saddam slaughter the Kurds and Shia. We forgot too soon who torched the Kuwaiti oilfields, who destroyed Kuwait, who wantonly polluted the Gulf. In an extraordinary switch of optical perspective,it seemed that Bush was to blame for the appalling endgame of the war, and not Saddam. He may have played the endgame callowly and callously and carelessly, but was he to blame in the same language that Saddam was clearly to blame?

We turned too soon onto the not very appealing Kuwaiti royal family for "not restoring democracy" immediately. True, sympathy ran out for them pretty fast, but the conditions of life in Kuwait were rather overlooked. Overwhelmingly, the critics of the war overlooked and continue to overlook this fact. Yes, its aftermath is messy, tragic and appalling – but look at what the consequences would have been if Saddam had not been fought and defeated?

It is too easy to point to what has gone wrong and ignore the almost certain consequences that would have followed inaction. What are they? To start with, the sanctions issue. I don't believe that anybody believes that sanctions could have worked, or at least in an acceptable time frame. Suppose that Saddam was vulnerable in three to five years' time – and look at the weak impact that continuing draconian sanctions are having, or not having, on the bomb-wrecked economy – where would we have got in that time? Saddam would have been able to chalk up the following plusses: he would have absorbed Kuwait, its territory peopled by Iraqis, its identity a thing of the past: his armed forces would be short of spare parts, though after three years someone would have sold him something, but they would be intact and boasting of a second successive victory; his championing of the Palestinians would have brought him increased and continuing credit in the Arab world; the PLO would have been strengthened by its association with such a champion; his nuclear and chemical armoury would be stronger, with those very same European firms who built it in the first place proving suitably complaisant in keeping it viable; the Kremlin military hardliners would feel delighted at the success of their client; is that enough?

Yes, the UN would have reverted to its former posture of weakness and ineffectiveness, willing to wound – sanctions – but still afraid to strike – to show a will and capability to act. One further thought springs to mind. Is it really conceivable that Israel would stand idly by and watch the West fail to muster the will and ability to restrain Saddam? It is an odds-on bet that within three years of the scenario set out above, Israel and Iraq would have been at war in the Mother of All Battles – and who would the Arabs have backed then? None of this is speculation – it is a plain recognition of the consequences of not fighting Saddam.

I have strayed from the question of our coverage to that of the war itself but there is a connection. Many of the critics of the coverage were also critics of the war itself. Because they disliked the war, they criticised the result by attacking the way it was reported. It is as if they believe that different reporting would – or at least should – have changed the outcome. For my part, there is one further area of coverage where we were slow – we did not latch on to the significance of the Reparations Resolution soon enough or monitor the difficulties of implementing it sufficiently. There is still time to put that right. We were distracted by the human impact of the Kurds, an extraordinary political event too, from charting the really profound implications of the Reparations Resolution and its implementation.

Yet these are all matters of editorial judgement rather than fundamental failures of method and system – human and personal – not institutional. In the final analysis, the systems put in place to report and analyse the war were not tested by the only thing that would have tested them – Allied defeats, or significant losses, or a reverse that cast doubt on the military strategy itself or a key part of it. How would we have responded then? My judgement is that we would have reported defeat or reverse as we did in WW2 – honestly and directly, because that is the only way you can report. A nation needs clear assessment and open debate when a war starts to go wrong. Casting doubt on a strategy that is failing is not a failure of patriotism, a sabotaging of the national will, a betrayal of the troops. It is rather the essential response needed to find a correct strategy. Persistence in error is a sin for a human being; it is not to be defended in governments. The troops deserve no less; they are the ones who die. To be sent to die for a wrong-headed strategy, or to continue to die in maintaining it, may be the prerogative of the super patriot – unlike the Patriot, the super patriot seldom hits its useful mark – but it should not be a tenable position for a journalist.

The next war will be covered both more fully and with a greater concern for subtlety, for causal analysis as well as futuristic speculation, for the difference between what we have been told, what we know, what we do not know and what is being deliberately withheld, and with a determination to report the bad news as well as the good. The armed forces are not protected by communiques that claim heavy casualties, and by policies which assert that they will be victorious when the evidence accumulates that they may be disastrous. The general public may prefer at times of national peril to put their heads in the sand; it saves no serviceman's life to take up that posture. Reporting a victory was comparatively easy. The criteria of reporting should be the same when the subject is imminent defeat. That should be the real lesson of the Gulf War.

CHAPTER 3
A VERY PARTICULAR EVIL
KUWAIT ONE YEAR ON

W EDNESDAY, JANUARY 29: Who could not be curious about Kuwait: that small patch of oil-filled desert sand which led the world to a rough awakening about the happy new world order, which gathered together the post-war's greatest military coalition and welded the U.N. into a new cohesion, gave us the first hi-tech war, the world's first live "as seen on tv" war, which started a hundred arguments about motives and morality: "If Kuwait had had carrots and not oil, the West would never have defended it"; "If Kuwait had had carrots and not oil, Saddam Hussein would never have invaded it." What is the place like? How destroyed is it? What are the scars of such a brutal occupation? – on that last question at least everybody can agree.

The political campaign for the visitor's heart and mind starts on the tarmac. The Kuwait Boeing 727 – "This has seen better days" says my English neighbour – has the slogan "Do not forget our POWs" painted in large letters on the fuselage. Is this the first political slogan ever painted on an aircraft's hull? Where will it stop? The plane from Dubai glides gently down over the bluest of blue waters, the Gulf, with fishing boats at their traditional work, looking tranquil beyond belief, the line between eternal sand and eternal sea clear and fundamental. The desert? A huge swathe of blackened sand running south east, the result of nine months' belching forth of oil-dark smoke from the 634 torched oil heads. (Torched, like gunned down, is one of those American toughtalk cliches, usually best avoided. In this instance the word is wholly appropriate.)

Will all the waters of Araby wash the stain away? Only the roads and tracks show through in their true desert colour like crease lines on a miner's face. Further on, the remains of a large oil tank farm, blackened and useless, the roof of all twelve tanks wrenched off, the whole made quite unserviceable. The devil of the Iraqui destruction was in its thoroughness. Lower and lower on the glide path to the airport, the scrape marks of gun emplacements appear, like the scratchings of an enormous, malign chicken. So far so bad, so far so predictable.

Then the surprises start. Kuwait was, after all, the place whose essential services had been destroyed by the Iraqis; whose goods, chattels had been stolen, pillaged or destroyed; whose families had been intimidated, raped, shot, tortured or deported. This was no ordinary occupation, except perhaps in its brevity. Surely the marks must, would show in all their pain and anguish. But the first impression is of an extraordinary normality. The airport terminal is spruce and integral in its white paint. Empty, certainly – a state in economic depression, yes – but not the entry point of a state almost destroyed by political vandalism. If this was the worst the Iraquis could do, they had a lot to learn from the Gestapo in Warsaw.

The first tell-tale sound outside the airport is the hum of the tyres of the American-built Mercury on the roads, a ribbed humming. This is due to the corrugation of the road surface by the Iraqui tanks, an aural reminder of the constant pounding of the surfaces by the Iraqui military presence. When the road markings are so clear, the white lines so immaculate, the bridges so freshly painted, you need the reminder of the tyre hum to create a sense of perspective. True, the Sheraton is still half-destroyed, it is clear the damage was inflicted thoroughly, systematically, room by room, the hotel operating from a new temporary entrance which must once have been the tradesmen's entrance. Opposite, the shopping mall of Al-Muthana is externally unscathed, inside its entire three floors are empty, while builders restore the shops, every one of the hundreds in the complex, to working order. You have to look for the damage now, the place is not filled with construction sites, scaffolding, builders' lorries. Kuwait has at least put a decent face on itself. No wrecked cars in the streets, no military relics, and the place looks as if it has been obsessively swept, with even sandy open car parks quite litter free. It is like a poor person, someone traumatised by shock, who is determined to keep up appearances; no one will see the tears or the strain behind the make-up, because the pancake has been applied too well, certainly too well to allow questioning.

Kuwait is not like Muscat, obsessively manicured and watered to the point of unreality – Hampstead Garden Suburb on the Gulf. My guide, Agab Al Zuaabi, observes that a car park now entirely filled with modern American and Japanese cars was covered with vandalised wrecks at liberation. "They took everything from the cars, even doors, instruments, steering wheels". He himself was in Kuwait throughout the occupation. He worked in a bakery – unheard of for a Kuwaiti. "We Kuwaitis learned a lot about ourselves. Everybody thought we were soft, loved only good living, shopping and having a nice time. In the occupation we surprised ourselves. Some collected garbage, others worked in bakeries. We found terrific energy and determination in ourselves. That is why the country recovered so fast afterwards and looks as it does." Is that energy and drive still there? "Yes, of course it is." On one occasion an Iraqui officer came into the bakery and ordered him to hand over 100 loaves of bread. Agab said he refused even when the officer put a gun to his head. "Get me an official order, and I will give you the bread. But there are people queueing here and they must have it before you". The officer went away.

At home on another occasion, the house was searched. First he hid his sub-machine gun in the cot of a newly born baby, then he shamed the Iraqui officer by saying it was customary to congratulate the mother who has just given birth. Too embarrassed by this involvement in human courtesy, the Iraqui took his search team away. Agab refuses to wear traditional dress until all the Kuwaiti hostages are freed from Iraq.

An hour after arrival from Dubai, after an uncomfortable overnight flight from London, I am with the Information Minister, Dr Bader Jassim al-Yaqoub. He rocks me back by asking for assistance in setting up a Kuwaiti World Service by February 24th. "The transmitters will be ready on that day and we want to broadcast three hours a day in English to the United States. My engineers say they will reach America." I am hardly up to this, jet-lagged and sleepless, but an agreement to look at their needs appears to satisfy honour all round. Clearly though, the broadcasting operation is starting from scratch. They have no journalists because most of them were "non-Kuwaiti nationals", an all too frequent euphemism for Palestinians who by and large made up the journalist/broadcaster class in the Gulf. Given that Kuwaitis recoil in loathing when they hear a Palestinian voice on our Arabic Service, their refusal to tolerate the accent on their own air waves is understandable. Professionally, the wound is vast.

To the temporary Palace set up in the buildings put up for the meeting of the GCC (Gulf Cooperation Council). Sheikh Nasser Al-Mohammed al-Sabah, Minister of Amiri Diwan Affairs, the Amir's chef de cabinet. He sits in a large, tented, curtained diwan, cell-phone on his lap, an adviser at his side, rather round, friendly, outgoing. Arabic cardamom coffee arrives, light brown, hardly coffee at all, the taste overwhelmed by the spice – a superb tonic and stimulant. Sweet Ceylon tea in a small glass cup soon follows. The French Finance Minister and entourage arrive en route to another meeting. Sheikh Nasser greets them effusively in French.

This is the business of the Diwan, the coming and going, the endless despatch of little business, the minute concern with small favours, the total knowledge of who has been to see whom and when, the world of the word in the right ear. One of the Diwan's advisers, Mohammed Sayed Ali Al-Rifaie talks of the Iraqi treatment of Kuwaitis in the occupation. One way of protecting the women from rape was to marry them off to almost anybody. It was a form of protection, he said. "Imagine a family with five daughters. If the Iraqis came there, all of the women would be raped. If they were all married, then the Iraquis would find only one woman at a time." He shrugged at the idea of the extraordinary things people have to do to avoid evil. There is too much Diwan business going on for a serious conversation with Sheikh Nasser, so I make my excuses and thanks and go to recover from the journey in the hotel.

Along the Gulf Road, the perfection of the Iraqui's destruction begins to emerge. The parliament may not be great shakes by western standards, but it was a whole lot better than anything Saddam had – the chamber was burned. So too was the Emir's palace, and the Crown Prince's clearly came in for some special attention. But there is something very special about invaders who gut beach cafes, seaside pleasure gardens, beach-side hotels. There is something trivial about such destruction, but at the same time deliberate and evil. Even in the average run of political evil, you should not systematically destroy the way a people enjoy themselves.

At 4 pm, Agab takes me to the Defence Minister, Sheikh Ali Al-Sabah, to his home. The Sheikh has invited me to join him as he puts in an appearance at half-a-dozen traditional Bedouin weddings. First we talk. He is slight, slim, very alert and quick on the uptake, very intelligent. His house has been rebuilt since the occupation; he wishes to keep several graffiti left behind by the Iraquis as a constant reminder of what happened. His wife just wants the place cleaned up and rebuilt. In this matter, it looks as if the Sheikh will have his way.

We talk of Saddam's mistakes, and the view, put forward by the US Defence Secretary Dick Cheney, that Saddam made two mistakes: the first was to invade Kuwait; the second was not to invade Saudi, because that would have denied Saudi allies the use of ports and airbases without which the coalition could never have assembled as it did and built up its forces. "I think that is right. I believed he should have gone as far as he could. It would have been far harder to liberate Saudi than to liberate Kuwait. He would have had many more options before him."

How powerful is Saddam now? "We call him the Mayor of Baghdad, because he doesn't control a lot outside. Recently we know that he withdrew all heavy equipment from units outside

Baghdad, leaving them only light fire arms. That means he does not trust them." He believes the Kuwaitis made one big mistake beforehand and the Allies one big one after the war. "We Kuwaitis were making a lot of noise in the Diwaniyahs talking politics, sounding as if we were divided. I believe Saddam misunderstood it. He thought that those who were making the criticism of the ruling family in the Diwaniyahs would support him and make a puppet government. When he got here, no Kuwaiti would touch it. But we gave him the wrong impression."

The Allies' mistake? "After the war Saddam was vulnerable. But once the Shia and Kurds started rebelling, the West helped them, and they made it clear that they were against not only Saddam but the whole of the Ba'ath Party. So, the Ba'ath supported Saddam because they had no choice."

We get into Sheikh Ali's Lincoln and drive across town to the North West. I comment on the extraordinary speed of Kuwait's reconstruction. "Yes, it is remarkable, but it may have been done too fast. Perhaps we needed to be reminded of what happened a little longer. Psychologically, it should not have been done so fast." We pass several tents brightly lit with lights, and these are all for wedding celebrations. "Almost every week, I have five or six to go to. But now so long as the Kuwaiti hostages are in Iraq, the ceremonies will be private and simple, but the public hospitality still takes place."

It is now very cold. Even in a wool suit, which I wear only because I had to wear it in the cold of London and flew out in the evening, I am shivering. The family rush out to greet the Sheikh as they see his car arrive. Much kissing three times on the cheek, the kiss on the shoulder of respect, congratulations to the groom – no women are present of course – and we all sit in a line in armchairs in an open tent, the floor carpeted with dozens of rugs. An incense holder is brought to the Sheikh, burning off a cloud of slightly acrid, slightly aromatic smoke. The glowing embers are of a special tree whose diseased wood emits this prized odour. You hold it below your chin and waft clouds of it at your face. It is not choking at all. Once the incense has moved down the line from the guest of honour's left, it returns to him so he gets a double helping before passing down to the right. The wood is quite rare and can be incredibly expensive, depending on quality.

After twenty minutes we leave, drive on a short distance to another wedding where the ritual is repeated. Here the faces are even more extraordinary: angle-featured, lined, sculptured, timeless in the kafiyah and dishdasha, anachronistically but sensibly wrapped in the occasional blanket or army style overcoat. The temperature must be six degrees Centigrade. In the summer it is forty degrees Centigrade or more. There is little attempt at conversation. The forms matter, and the forms are being observed. (Is it a Western obsession to talk, regardless of the substance or the need? Why are we so restless with silence?) The Minister of the Interior arrives. Two Ministers represents a big honour. I have to get back to dinner with the Ambassador, so I thank him sincerely for a fascinating couple of hours and make for the warmth of the car and hotel.

Dinner in Michael Weston's residence, a fine old colonial building, semi-circular, brick-built, with the rooms opening off a circular staircase, and open fires burning logs in the sitting room. One of the oldest buildings in Kuwait, formerly the British Agent's residence. It must have been imposing in comparison then. An interesting gathering: Anthony Parsons and wife are here lecturing, he is as sharply intelligent as ever, she one of those marvellous dip/empire wives, direct, no nonsense, very funny. A very able Kuwaiti political scientist, formerly head of the University; a newspaper editor (Al-Fajer Al- Jadid) and occasional tv interviewer, who is to interview me the next day, Jassem Al-Qabarzad, a member of the KNC and one of the leading London-based spokesmen for the Free Kuwait Movement during the occupation, a senior Kuwaiti FO man and member of the Royal Family (Michael Weston apologises for the fact that both FM and Deputy FM are abroad), Mrs Amal Al-Hamad and so on.

Tony Parsons, the political scientist and I discuss the absence of a political uprising by the "Arab masses" in support of Saddam Hussein as was widely predicted. Parsons admits that he warned a London audience before the fighting that once Britons and Americans started shooting Arabs, then the "masses would rise up from Morocco to Saudi and sweep away the governments that supported them". The political scientist agreed that Arab states were now successful as states but still unsuccessful as nations. Therein lay their dilemma. All agreed that the Palestinians were heartily disliked by their fellow Arabs – that during the Israeli attack on Beirut, for instance, Arab governments were recoiling from supporting the PLO.

Over dinner, the discussion gets very heavy with a debate on the definitions, uses and abuses of the word "terrorism" including the nuances, political and linguistic, of the word in English and Arabic. Feelings are in danger of getting slightly out of hand, but they confirm my long-held view that the word should be used only sparingly because it is such a strong one, and should not be used as an automatic Homeric epithet in order to denote permanent and habitual condemnation. Once a word has become so encumbered with assumptions and emotional overloading, it has ceased to be a useful at all. Its use probably obstructs understanding rather than the reverse.

Over coffee, we get cracking on the really hard stuff – "Zionism". The political scientist demonstrates that Zionism is objectionable because it is exclusive, and therefore not conducive to tolerance and civil rights. I do not disagree but state my point that fifteen years of UN branding of Israeli Zionism as being "racist" has had absolutely zero effect on that country's policies. Arguably the resolution only gave the real Zionists ammunition to argue that accommodation with the Arabs was a fantasy because of the extremism of their condemnation. So much for political name-calling and label-tagging; they militate against understanding, and probably obstruct agreement which is hard enough to achieve at the best of times.

Thursday, January 30. Something of the atmosphere of the

evening's discussion rubs off onto the morning meeting. It is Desert Storm weather, a fierce desert wind blowing fine dust in thick clouds everywhere. Visibility is like a thickish fog, the palm trees are bending in the wind's force, your mouth fills with fine grit after a few seconds. No wonder the allied commanders dreaded the winter sandstorms.

I visit the Under Secretary for Radio in the Ministry of Information, who asks for assistance in training broadcasters, technicians, television producers, administrators, in Kuwait as soon as possible. The scale of the request is jolting, but so is the failure to admit its reason – the expulsion/departure of the Palestinians – sorry "non-Kuwaitis" – who ran broadcasting before. I say that when we know the scale of the task, we can no doubt suggest some former members of the Arabic Service who would be interested in coming over to do some contract training. But: "No, that would not be right. We know the Arabic Service were in favour of Saddam Hussein in the war".

There is something about the bald assertion that the bias was unquestionable that riles me at 9.30 in the morning. I reel off what we did to supervise the Arabic broadcasts, deny his vague accusations, and try to close the matter. He then asserts that most of the Service are Palestinian and ignores my reply that it includes eighteen nationalities and the largest group is Egyptian. I am in real danger of losing my temper but decide that would be a bad idea and ask him merely to send us a detailed list of requirements which we will study. I reflect on the irony of the fact that in November, I was berated by Nigerians for a week about our coverage being allegedly too anti-Saddam, and now two months later, the accusation is in the reverse but equally passionately held. I doubt if I will ever find an answer but take comfort in the thought – if it is comfortable – that everybody listens with total subjectivity.

My next visit is better, Yousef al Sumait, new Chairman of the state news agency, KUNA. The offices are newly carpeted, newly decorated. The furniture is new, some still crated up. The corridor leading to his office is lined with large floral decorations, sent to him on his arrival in the job just three days ago. He gestures disarmingly, openly. "I have nothing, no organisation, no structure, no communications, no administration, no trained staff. I start from nothing." From him, the request for help sounded decent, my inability to do anything about it a matter of real regret.

Has the occupation changed Kuwaitis? "I wish I felt that Kuwaitis had learned a sense of responsibility from this. I am not sure. The other day there was a letter in the paper saying that the government should pay the electricity bills! Is that taking responsibility?" He shrugs doubtfully. We tour the premises. The shock between what there is and what there was is huge. The office has all the mod cons of luxury – new carpets, desks and paint – but remains a useless husk. The Iraquis ripped out everything; the archives destroyed; photo archives almost totally destroyed, but one filing cabinet was recovered from Baghdad, the negatives so distorted by exposure to the desert that they are probably unusable; the communications control centre, a web of intricate connections had had all the wiring deliberately, systematically cut – it must have taken hours to do it, probably with nail scissors; all the agency machines were removed, and a few score were returned, but only those that had needed repairing in the first place; in one room a group of engineers and technicians are conferring about the huge task of restoration and rehabilitation. So like much of Kuwait, the exterior is restored, but the inside of the institution is empty. It takes a very special effort to remove everything that makes a news agency work, a very special eye for detail, a very special wish to render things unusable for a very long time; it is not casual vandalism but systematic and planned and driven by a particular hatred. One day the Kuwaitis may get round to thinking about the origins of this complex hatred, and perhaps scrutiny might only dignify it, but the time is a long way away.

The National Museum next. A small, lean, scurrying, jack rabbit Director, Dr Fahed al-Wohabi, voluble, professional and unsentimental. Just as well. His heart would have been broken otherwise. Outwardly the fine, modern, French designed buildings are largely unmarked, disfigured only by the occasional scorch mark, as if there had been a local fire inside, easily put out. The reality is, even by Kuwait's standards, appalling. Three of the buildings were utterly scorched by fire, every wall, every ceiling, charred to unrecognisability. The objects were either stolen – some later returned – but the paintings of Kuwait's best contemporary painters were simply piled up and burned to cinders. A huge collection of Islamic art was pillaged, a huge wooden thirteenth century door burned because it was too large to move.

The director only tells us about the research floor. All the research manuscripts, including his archaeological papers of his own digs, were burned to ashes. Dr Fahed says with anguished simplicity that he can still see the remains of his own research among the ashes, but apologises for not taking me up to see it on grounds that the building is not safe.

We go to the planetarium. "In Baghdad they have an identical planetarium to this one. Here we had various displays about outer space that they did not have. If they had stolen our equipment and our computer software for the programmes for their planetarium, I could almost understand it. But no, they worked really hard to destroy this one. Here are two places where they started fires but they didn't catch, so they really had to put a lot of effort into burning the auditorium." Sure enough like the rest of the museum, it is charred and burned in detail. There is something especially horrible about an attack on a museum, worse even than burning books – there are almost certainly other copies – it is an assault on knowledge, on thought, on reflection, on ideas, on any attempt to recapture the past and through it to place order and meaning on the present. It signals total contempt for the attacked and their human claim to identity and the graces that constitute civilisation. Anything more than the basics of existence was trampled down. Dr Fahed says: "When we rebuild, we will keep part of the destruction as a reminder". We scuttle through the cold driving rain to a large patch of ashes. "Here we had the last working dhow on display. It is our national symbol. It is on our coins. They burned it."

In the afternoon, it is windy, cold and sand blasted as we drive to the National Display Centre. Its car park contains a display of war booty. I photograph the Soviet-built tanks, armoured personnel carriers, guns, howitzers, mortars, a Scud launcher, multiple machine guns, anti-aircraft guns. None was destroyed; all these were abandoned. I shoot off my film, and the officer accompanying us says he will just take us to see a few more. It is breathtaking, a whole army-full of equipment lined up over several acres, neatly parked, drawn up almost as if it were a military parade. How many? Perhaps 500 tanks, and at least as many APCs and heavy guns. It was an armada for Armageddon.

I am late back to the hotel to do a tv interview for Jassem Al-Qabarzard. "Oh yes, the Iraquis had many ways of stealing. Sometimes they said 'Give us the car keys or we shoot you'. They liked Land Rovers and 4WD vehicles in particular. Or they would say 'We want to buy this car, here is the receipt'. If you said where is the money, they said 'Go to the police station, the officer will pay you'. If they stole equipment, it was in order to repair it, if they stole art it was to protect it. Oh yes, they had thought about the art of stealing a lot."

I record almost an hour for Jassem and get to evening drinks with assorted westerners rather late. Gossip is lively. What does the Opposition want from reform? "Basically they want to be able to appoint the Prime Minister. They want to stop the system by which the Crown Prince is also the Prime Minister. But they don't realise that Kuwaiti governments don't take decisions. They talk and talk; most problems simply go away; the others may crawl through to a consensus. But they do not take decisions."

The question arises whether the Kuwaitis can stand a reduction of the population and the economy – the Kuwaitis were 28% of the population, now they plan to represent 60% of it. Does this amount to a savage contraction of the economy? "It would if it was a normal economy. But nature gave the Kuwaitis oil which emerges at 100 feet above sea level, all they have to do is to run it towards the sea and they are rich. A normal economy with taxation and economic activity simply does not need to operate. Of course, the merchants will have fewer people to sell durables to, but that won't matter a lot".

Still on the Crown Prince: "A nice man but quite incapable of taking a decision. His father said of him that he couldn't even decide which one of thirty identical dishdasha he should put on in the morning". On the state of mind of the Amir: "Saddam took Jaabar aside and said: 'There are many plots to kill me. If I am killed, I want you, my brother Jaabar, to look after my family'. The Amir took this as the supreme expression of trust. The invasion then simply destroyed all those assumptions."

Friday, January 31. The sandstorm is almost blown out. The sky is blue-ish, the sun peers through, the temperature is warm. I go off to tour the oil fields. The sand is blackened where the smoke fell in oily globules. Elsewhere it has formed a thick crust three inches thick. At the Ahmidy Governorate the police station is destroyed, so is the Governor's administrative offices. So were the pipelines. So were the offices of the Kuwait Oil Company. So were the oil gathering stations, their twisted forms strangely but comfortlessly like an Anthony Caro sculpture. They reflect a dehumanised mind in action. The cost of reconstructing the oilfield is estimated at $75 billion. Here there is a huge junkyard of twisted metal from destroyed installations. There are vast vehicle parks of lorries, bulldozers and cranes used to put out the fires.

Amazingly, a lark rises from a desolate scrub and sings as if it were on Salisbury Plain, singing amid the oil lakes, product of the effortless gushing of the oil after the fires had been put out before the well heads had been capped. The largest lake stretches for at least a quarter of a mile in each direction. Thick, dark, viscous, it will take six months to pump out to the tank farms for collection and then for cheap sale because of its pollution.

Even the desert will suffer for years because its top soil was heavily impacted by the Iraqui tank tracks. Here and there a destroyed Iraqui tank or APC. One of them stands in a pool of oil, symbol of our utter failure and the pointlessness of the whole venture. In Bahrain, a Kuwaiti financier tells me that the total cost of the two Gulf wars to the Gulf states has been $500 billion. How can we be so stupid? The burning of the oil wells was so deliberately evil, the extinction of the fires so heroic, so much better than we deserved, we still have not truly come to terms with either.

Written during a visit to Kuwait, 29-31 January, 1992

CHAPTER 4
TRUTH SAVES LIVES
COMMUNICATION & POLITICS

THE VERY IDEA that telling the truth in government and public affairs is the best policy must sound hopelessly unrealistic and idealistic. Public communications have become something to capture, to influence and to manipulate. Either they are captured by the great Moguls of the media – the Murdochs in America and Britain, the Bertelsmanns in Germany, the Berlusconis in Italy, whose interest in the control of the means of distribution are directly financial, and who have, more often than not, a political line to put over, or they are captured and seized by politicians who of course always have a clear political line to put over.

In a totalitarian state, the control of communications lies at the heart of the methods by which political power is established and maintained. The disastrous results that follow are there for all to see. But neither are democracies simon-pure in this respect. Even in a democracy, the prevailing political line of the party in office influences the picture of events which society has. Politicians deploy the whole panoply of media devices:

The Unattributable Briefing: ("you can say what I tell you, but don't say I told you").

The Deniable Statement: ("even if you do say I told you, I will say that I didn't, that you misquoted me, I did not know your tape recorder was still running or our back-up tape recording of the interview hasn't worked").

The Leak: (if it comes from a junior civil servant, they may be prosecuted; if from a senior one and it has the intended effect, they may well be promoted. Hence the well known declension, "I brief, you leak, he gets prosecuted").

The Well Flown Kite: ("yes, such ideas have been aired in the

Ministry but there is not the slightest chance of their becoming policy"); this actually means that the reaction to the kite flying was so violent that the policy has actually been scrapped

It is Not Policy at Present: meaning that it may become policy next week.

The whole dreary world which has turned too much public information into media manipulation was memorably summed up by the misfired attempt at irony by the most senior civil servant in Britain, the Cabinet Secretary Sir Robert Armstrong. In the course of the British government's long and finally unsuccessful attempt to suppress Peter Wright's *Spycatcher* book in Australia, he admitted to having been "economical with the truth" – a phrase borrowed from Edmund Burke which has now become firmly if oh so unintentionally rooted in the English canon of popular reference, 200 years after it was first coined.

Fortunately there is more to communications than a cynical world of half-truths and whole lies. An increasing body of modern experience lends support to the contention that in the field of communications and politics, telling the truth is the best policy a government can adopt. What Abraham Lincoln might have added to his observation "You can fool all of the people some of the time, and some of the people all of the time" was that in the course of attempting to fool all the people all the time, governments are usually the first victims of their deception. Satisfyingly appropriate as this feels, the tragedy of such institutional self-deception is that it usually leads to the death of innocent civilians as a direct result. There is good evidence and growing belief in the fact that even in today's wicked world, morality and politics can march comfortably hand in hand.

The evidence for this claim is drawn from different continents and societies; one deals with famine, the other with freedom. The television images of famine in Ethiopia, brought first by John Osman in 1975, then by Michael Buerk in 1984, seared themselves on all viewers' eyes. Associated with those images of deprivation and death were other images – those of the relief agencies, mainly western, always compassionate and professional, detached yet committed, technicians of life and community support, and often identified with such attractive committed, plausible and diverse figures as Princess Anne and Bob Geldof. The direct or strongly implied message from this coverage – the suffering and the relief, the helpless and the helpers, the victims and the carers – has been that African governments cannot by themselves prevent famine – indeed by their own actions, which all too often lead to war or civil war, they actively create it – and that outside relief agencies have to sort out the mess and almost alone can do so.

A recent book, *Hunger and Public Action* by two distinguished economists, Professors Dreze and Sen, calls this stark, antithetical view into question. Their thesis is that a free media and active participatory politics have a direct and beneficial impact on the prevention of and solution of famines.

Put simply, free speech saves lives. Let us examine this by considering the images of governmental inaction and relief agency action that are so prevalent. Who can forget the Live Aid Concert at Wembley in 1985 and its huge appeal of "Feed the World"? Well, did it feed the world? Did it change anything in Africa? Did the movement itself achieve anything that other aid agencies had not achieved or had attempted and failed? The answer to all three questions is no, no and no.

To make that reply is not to decry the spirit or the decent impulses behind that movement, still less to put off anyone who gives aid to such charities. They are vitally important, and undoubtedly effective in the immediate relief of hunger and the long-term supply of training and the prevention of famine. Yet their role in such activities may be less important than the action of individual governments, unreported as they may often be. For, according to Professors Dreze and Sen, there is no need to be too depressed – hunger in Africa is often overcome, but those victories attract less attention than they should and it is overcome by positive action by good governments.

The authors list at least eleven countries in Africa where famines have, over the years, been quietly and effectively relieved by the governments concerned. They conclude that one of the factors helping either to prevent famine or allowing governments to act rapidly to remedy it, is the operation of the media in their role "as conveyors of information and as organs of public criticism and advocacy". Dreze and Sen add: "Adversarial politics forces an early response from the government in power in the event of a crisis. The interest that a political opposition has to find out, disseminate and use information about an impending food crisis can make a crucial difference, if the opposition is allowed to function".

In Zimbabwe between 1982-4, the press took a sharply adversarial stance against the government. They campaigned regularly about hardship and malnutrition in the countryside, reported parliamentary debates on the subject and exposed profiteering. In the four countries in Africa where famine has been successfully overcome, three have an active and largely uncensored press.

The authors do not regard this as a coincidence. Free media are certainly not a sufficient condition for defeating famine but they are almost certainly a necessary condition. It is an encouraging idea that while political pluralism, some brand of democracy aided and supported by free media may be inconvenient, untidy, obstreperous and a thorough nuisance – the worst form of government, said Winston Churchill, except all the others – yet a government which suppresses pluralism and the information that it throws up is far less likely to relieve famine and far more likely to kill its citizens. Oppositions are often criticised by ruling parties for making political capital out of human misfortune. It is their function and their responsibility to make a political issue out of human misfortune, for if they do not, then the human suffering is usually far greater still.

This bold thesis is thoroughly tested by Professors Dreze and Sen in their examination of two starkly contrasted famines in very differently organised societies – India and China. For decades, economists have disputed over the political and economic virtues of China and India. Which was the superior in providing its people with a decent standard of living? China, with its tight political control, its draconian policies for birth control, its mass mobilisation programmes for rural works? Or India, with its diverse, diffuse responses to need because no government can second-guess consumer choices – no matter at however basic a level?

India has endured well publicised difficulties with food supply but it will surprise many that it has had no famine since Independence in 1947. Hunger, yes, shortages, suffering, of course, but not actual famine. It is in the authors' view even more striking, given the frequency of droughts and floods and acute shortages of food. The reason that they did not become actual famine was because the Indian political system acted as a trigger, an early warning system and a spur to government action. In other words, it worked as a political system should. Indian governments were alerted earlier to the imminence of famine; their press and opposition politicians told them of it. Their governments acted sooner and more decisively because it would have been politically unwise not to do so – quite apart from any thoughts of humanity. "The adversarial participation of newspapers and opposition leaders is an important part of the famine prevention system," according to the academics.

The contrast with China's famine between 1958-61 could not be more striking. It is now estimated that between 16 and 30 million Chinese died in these years of Chairman Mao's 'Great Leap Forward'. This great forced march towards industrialisation was highly lauded internationally. It tended to be taken at face value – a face elaborately applied by the Chinese authorities. Yet for three years, the reality was that Chinese food production and distribution had collapsed. It was not merely that this fact was concealed from the outside world. The 'Great Leap Forward' was one of the most successfully promoted political movements in a generation. In the West, it was virtually unthinkable to criticise it or cast doubt on its deep wisdom and assured efficacy. This was possible because of the total control of information and political discussion possessed by the Chinese Communist Party. But this control, while tempo-rarily flattering for their rulers, had tragic consequences for China's people. Local Chinese party officials feared to tell their superiors what was actually happening because their experience not only revealed their own failure, but conflicted with the picture painted by official statistics. These boasted of huge national grain stocks – the statistics could not contradict the party line which was that the party's agricultural policies were a triumphant success. Because the Chinese leaders were convinced by their own statistics, they not only believed in the existence of vast grain stores, but reduced food imports to zero. Worse still, the Chinese government increased the volume of grain for export – while millions of their citizens were not merely hungry but were actually dying. At that time, China was totally led and directed by a Communist Party which shut out dissent, disagreement or any alternative view. The seeds of the attitudes which led to the mass hysteria of the Red Guards and their slavish devotion to the banalities of Chairman Mao's Little Red Book were already present. Professors Dreze and Sen assert unequivocally that the blame for the Chinese famine can be attributed directly to China's lack of a "political system of advers-arial journalism and opposition". It is a terrible indictment. Governments who suppress essential facts kill their people because they have first fooled themselves.

This is not to imply that the manner in which information is spread in Britain is ideal – far from it. Government departments are ludicrously secretive, far more so than their counterparts in the United States. The official attitude towards the media in the United States is strikingly different. They have a Freedom of Information Act and the press is recognised as the Fourth Estate with a positive duty to let the citizen know. In Britain we are governed through a distrust of public information, and journalists are almost at the bottom of the list of esteemed professions. So long as Britain has regulations such as the ban on broadcasting the voices of members of para-military organisations in Northern Ireland, it will not be able to adopt a holier-than-thou attitude to others.

But there is another country and another area where the price of telling lies has proved a hideous one – the Soviet Union. The chief agent which produced the destructive political reaction which blew the USSR apart was the previously novel practice of telling the truth. "Glasnost" simply means openness – not a difficult idea in itself. But the devastating impact of glasnost can only be explained by the fact that it was let loose on a system which had been run for the previous seven decades on lies. It is worth examining what former Soviet officials now say about the consequences of news control. Take the speed – or rather the delays – with which they habitually reported major events. The head of State Radio and Television, Leonid Kravchenko, recalled the shooting down of the Korean airliner, KAL 007 by Soviet jet fighters in 1983 and its announcement on the Soviet news media. By that time, all the rest of the world knew of it and most of the Soviet Union did too, because the Soviet citizens were either listening to the foreign radios, such as the BBC World Service, or were getting news from friends who did. The delay was ridiculous and self defeating.

Just over a year ago, an article in *Pravda*, the Soviet Communist Party official newspaper, lamented the fact that they had delayed reporting news of the Soviet invasion of Afghanistan. The author wrote in April 1989: "we journalists and international affairs experts knew in the editorial office that an 'important event' was going to take place that day. It was only in the evening that we received a *Tass* report on the Afghan government request to send troops to that country. It was published in *Pravda* the following day. But, the day before that happened, the teletype rooms of Western news agencies were literally delirious, painting all the details of the events of which the readers learned many hours later. Our version hit the world when public opinion was already prepared – and not inclined in our favour".

Now there's more to that thought than the canny observation of a journalistic professional who understands that it is best to get your story in first: the Soviet Union would have lost the propaganda war over Afghanistan in the long-run even if Pravda had miraculously broken the news first, because the decision was disastrously wrong. It failed militarily and it set back Soviet-American relations for five years; the Soviets concede as much and President Gorbachev's decision to withdraw amounted to an official admission that it was a mistake. In this specific instance the implications of not telling the truth go deeper. The decision to invade was taken by a secluded leadership, operating in a closed political system, with the co-operation of a servile press. In February 1989, Valentin Falin, then head of the Soviet Central Committee's International department, was reported on Moscow Radio's World Service as making this comment on the lessons to be learned from the decision to enter Afghanistan. "Our tragedy in the past" he said, "was that many decisions were taken either by individuals or by groups of people behind closed doors. Often both the party and the government were excluded from decision-making. Many decisions were prompted by caprices of some leaders". In other words, the entire communist system, even in its own terms, broke down when it came to formulating a sensible policy over Afghanistan, deteriorating into mere leadership by whim. But their media allowed it to happen.

But the rot was more profound still. It is not as if some, perhaps many, influential people in the Soviet Union did not know better. In September 1990, a leading Soviet thinker on international affairs, Oleg Bogomolov, wrote a devastatingly candid article on this subject in the outspoken magazine *Ogonek*. Bogomolov called his article "I cannot absolve myself from guilt." He had strongly advised the Brezhnev leadership against sending Soviet troops to Afghanistan. "The invasion of Afghanistan might have never happened if those who in 1968 objected inwardly to the crushing of the Prague Spring had spoken out and acted openly". But inward objections were not enough; they must be spoken, expressed, reported. We should, wrote Bogomolov, have "protested openly against the deceit, the lies, and the violence". Once again, the Brezhnev leadership successfully kept the truth from their people. But apart from killing a hundred thousand Soviet troops needlessly, and deepening the tensions and miseries of the Cold War, they led their country into a diplomatically disastrous dead-end. Perhaps Bogomolov accused himself too much; there are policy-makers aplenty in western democracies who wonder why they did not go public with their anxieties about government policies. It is not as if great functioning democracies such as the United States do not make spectacular foreign policy errors. But the evidence continues to grow that the totality of the Soviet failure in so many areas sprang from the totalitarian nature of the system which suppressed the truth.

In May 1989, the leading official Soviet literary magazine, *Literaturnaya Gazeta* carried an article on the stagnation of public debate within the Soviet Union. The academic author wrote: "You will not find even a single mention of the slightest mistake or error in books or articles about our foreign policy. No matter what was done, everything is depicted as infallible. Of course Soviet foreign policy enjoys high esteem. But was everything done correctly?"

The soul searching in the former Soviet Union has continued in an anguished way. It records the way that government statistics were systematically falsified. Former President Gorbachev revealed that the existence of a huge budget deficit was painstakingly hidden from the public.

The contrast with the huge United States' budget deficit is striking. There the debate has been regular, open, candid and conducted in the full knowledge of the government's responsibilities for the deficit, as well as a full understanding of what the political and economic consequences are. One of the most radical new economic thinkers in the Soviet Union, Abel Agenbegyan, wrote in his recent autobiography of the moment when the full truth dawned about the state of the Soviet economy – it was only in January 1987 but Agenbegyan's conclusion will sound awfully familiar:

It was at this Plenum that we clearly understood that the main, the most profound, reason for the deformation of socialist society, for the failure of economic reforms and other progressive initiatives, lay in a lack of democracy, the way decisions were taken behind closed doors, and in the absence of any kind of control over the activity of the country's leaders.

There were other absurdities, such as the fictitious crime figures: while Britain claims a clear-up rate of crime of 18%, the official Soviet clear-up rate in some departments was officially stated to be 100.1%. Such ludicrous examples of the official mind became the stock in trade of Soviet journalism under Brezhnev, but by then it was too late.

The whole sorry picture of institutional self- disinformation, unwitting and therefore destructive, is crystallised in two articles by well-known Soviet figures. One is by Vitaly Korotich, editor of the above-mentioned *Ogonek*. Today *Ogonek* is, as it has been for the past two or three years, the darling of the Western press. It is glasnost personified, and its exposure of the problems of Soviet society and the failure of the successor government to solve them are profound, searching and effective. Korotich is charming, humorous, and clearly a good journalist. However I recently came across an article by Korotich from the *Literary Gazette*. It was written a mere six years ago, and I confess it shocked me. Not because it was an attack on the BBC Russian Service entitled "Pulsating Nucleus of Hatred" – there have been plenty of those over the years – but because of the nature of the attack. Many of the reports from the BBC Russian Service which Korotich rejected vehemently as "lies" in 1986 are undoubtedly issues which he might write about himself today in his paper. But it was the sheer nastiness of the tone which took me by surprise. Korotich's article ended:

Sometimes BBC people behave like mongooses striving to destroy everything snakelike, like ferocious and exclusive exterminators of everything it is their job to combat. But whereas the mongoose's hatred is ultimately of use to people, the hatred of unobjective propagandists engenders chauvinism. The arrogation of the exclusive right to judge, pardon, execute and sentence are throwbacks to bygone days and the black sails of British pirate admirals or the thick soles of colonists' shoes churning the dust on foreign roads.

There are several things to say about that. First, it is well written. Second, it is a period classic of its kind – a certain class of Cold War rhetoric. Third, the Soviet Union has come a long way in six years. And fourth, I don't criticise Korotich for writing as he did. But given what he writes now, what a deadly system it must have been to turn him as we now know him capable of being into the journalist who wrote that piece.

Korotich is not alone or exceptional. One of the most persuasive defenders of the official Soviet line over the years was the American-educated Vladimir Posner. In 1976, he attacked the nuclear physicist and dissident Andrey Sakharov as "the would-be Messiah-martyr Andrei Sakharov". Posner backed the official charge that the frail seventy-year-old had assaulted a police officer outside a court room in Omsk. Yet on the last page of his book published two years ago Posner wrote: "the spectacle of Andrei Sakharov standing his ground and speaking his mind gave me hope". Such reconstruction of attitudes is rather hard to take.

But there are statements which leave an altogether more pleasant taste in the mouth. One came in a short talk on Soviet television given by one of Mr. Gorbachev's closest advisers, Aleksandr Yakovlev. He spoke, quite briefly, on the day when President Gorbachev signed two decrees – one restoring rights to those persecuted by the Communist Party between 1920 and the 1950s. The second, restoring citizenship rights to those who had lost them because of alleged acts of dissidence, or as Yakovlev bluntly put it, "for freedom of thought".

In Soviet-speak, these people were being rehabilitated. In the past, anybody who was lucky enough to be alive when they were rehabilitated – and most of the victims of Stalinism remain firmly dead and unrehabilitated – would have thought the Communist

Party profoundly wise and generous to have reversed its previous sentence and verdict. Yakovlev's comment therefore must be seen in that context, in the fact that he is who he is, and in the fact that he appeared on prime time Soviet television to say it:

> *When we say we are rehabilitating somebody, as it were graciously forgiving them for certain errors of past years, all this, it seems to me, smacks of hypocrisy. It is not them we are forgiving, but ourselves. It is we who are to blame for the fact that they lived for years slandered and crushed. And we are rehabilitating ourselves, and not those who thought differently from us or who had other thoughts and convictions. They wished us merely good and freedom, but the state responded with the evil of the prisons and the camps.*

As if that were not enough, Aleksandr Yakovlev ended by confronting his television audience with this question: "How far has our society come in the difficult comprehension of truth, good and humanism?"

In that moving confrontation of the moral dilemma lying before the Soviet Union as it attempts to construct an open, civic society from the ruins of a closed, ideological society, Yakovlev articulated, with admirable directness, the nature of the problems that accumulate when society does not tell itself the truth.

I have dwelt on the experience of the Soviet Union because it is so intense, the consequences of institutionalised lie-telling so glaring, so final, so total, and the candour and anguish of the Soviet debate about it so deep, so very Russian. But let us be clear: openness and telling the truth will not prevent idiocy, although they ensure that problems are publicised and probably stand a better chance of being solved.

In the west, there is no room for complacency. As we look at the example of a society which lied to itself and destroyed itself in the process, we in Britain, with all the freedom of the media that we have, cannot stand on the corner of the open street and pray like the Pharisee "I thank you, Lord, that I am not as other men".

Instead, we should be properly cautious about how we point the finger and, to borrow from the New Testament again, first cast out the beam from our own eye.

First delivered at Leighton Park School 27 November 1990

CHAPTER 5

VOICES IN THE DARK

INTERNATIONAL BROADCASTING AND THE EUROPEAN REVOLUTIONS OF 1989

I T IS STILL hard to believe that the Revolutions of Autumn 1989 happened; difficult to comprehend that the Cold War is over: Marxism-Leninism discredited and abandoned as a practical way of running a state, let alone an economy, Comecon relegated to a mere clearing house for economic negotiation with the European Community, and the Warsaw Pact just a ghastly memory of the days when stirrings of political change in Eastern Europe were snuffed out by the inevitable arrival of the Red Army's tanks with a few dragooned allies in tow. As Czechoslovakia's playwright President, Vaclav Havel, said to the United States Congress on February 21, 1990: "The mask fell away so rapidly that we have literally no time even to be astonished".

But despite the insistent and alarming distractions of the Gulf, the new and ugly face of post-Cold War politics, let us take time to be "astonished". In all the celebrations of, and examinations into, the meaning of the French Revolution of 1789, nobody even bothered to speculate that two hundred years later, Europe might produce another revolution. I do not know of anyone who watched the Berlin Wall come down on television and did not weep. All of us who saw it come down are very lucky. Those of us who have lived through the starting of the Cold War forty years ago, who experienced the building of the Berlin Wall, who lived with the threatening and apparently immovable force of Soviet totalitarianism are even luckier – unimaginably so. I myself walked through the Brandenburg Gate as a national serviceman in Germany in 1955, looked with disbelieving horror at the wall and the deadly no-man's land beyond it in the 1960s, passed through the sadistically thorough security checks of Checkpoint Charlie or the Friedrichsstrasse railway station in the 1970s, and then drove through it again this May, when the Saxon border guards masked their fear and apprehension of the impending new Germany with a well-rehearsed set of forced smiles that were almost as chilling as their previous hostility. Writing in the February issue of *Granta*, the quarterly magazine published in Cambridge, Stephen Spender begins his reflections on Europe, Christmas Eve 1989, like this:

> *What is happening today ... has the effect of making me feel that I am witnessing apocalyptic events out of the Book of Revelations. For the collapse of the totalitarian regimes is something that I had given up hope of witnessing in my lifetime.*

In that same edition of *Granta*, the philosopher, Isaiah Berlin also reminded his readers of the emotional wonder of what has happened:

> *When men and women imprisoned for a long time by oppressive and brutal regimes are able to break free, at any rate from some of their chains, and after many years know even the beginnings of genuine freedom, how can anyone with the smallest spark of human feeling not be profoundly moved?*

You do not have to be aged eighty to respond like that. A friend of mine in his fifties was for several years the West German Representative in East Germany – their Ambassador in all but name. As he prepared to take up his next posting in the United Nations, a journalist asked him how he judged the chances of German Unification? My friend replied: "I walked through the Brandenburg Gate once in my life in 1960. I hope to walk through it once more before I die". Well, he needn't worry; he has done so.

None of this is to underestimate the scale of the difficulties that Europe as a whole now faces as it attempts to manage the transition between totalitarianism and hoped-for democracy. That is for the future. For the present, let us examine one possible factor of a whole array which forced the mask of totalitarianism to – as Vaclav Havel put it – "slip away". What was the impact made by those "Voices in the Dark" as they were called, the foreign radio stations such as Radio Free Europe, Radio Liberty, Voice of America, Deutsche Welle, and, of course, the BBC World Service? How did we keep minds open in closed societies? How did we – or did we even – open minds once closed? The full story has yet to be told, but there are already one or two instances that throw light on the process. Here is one authentic voice. It reached the BBC World Service in February 1990 in a letter from Romanian Moldavia:

> I have persistently listened to your broadcasts, many times hidden under a blanket in my monastic cell… I am convinced you made an important contribution to what we Romanians are experiencing today.

It is almost irresistible to be drawn into a falsely romantic picture of the letter writer – a monk in a medieval stone cell, with wall icons painted by a Romanian Andrei Rublev, pale, devout, other worldly. Well, perhaps he was. But I have no doubt that listening to the BBC Romanian Service in those years was dangerous to a degree we cannot begin to imagine. What sort of need drove millions to take the risks of listening to forbidden voices? First, what could these listeners, who really needed to know, hear on their radios?

For most of the last fifty years, we have been broadcasting in ten languages to the Soviet bloc – Bulgarian, Czech, Hungarian, Polish, Romanian, Russian, Serbo-Croat, Slovak, Slovene, and of course English. Important as the latter is as a global language, its role in the political dialogue with Eastern Europe during the Cold War has been interesting but marginal. If the BBC World Service had an impact, then it was principally through the broadcasts in the local, national language. Throughout the world English-speaking audiences are always smaller than those in the local national language, and their size is increased and maintained by the existence of our broadcasts in the national language as well.

The duration of the broadcasts varies considerably from six and a half hours of Russian per day, three and a half hours of Polish, to just under an hour per day of Slovene. [1990 figures] Important as this broadcasting effort is, it remains small by comparison with our western competitors. The United States, through its two stations the Voice of America and Radio Free Europe for Eastern Europe, and Radio Liberty for the Soviet Union, broadcasts six times as many hours in Russian, six times as much in Polish, and six times as much in Romanian. [1990 figures] Yet the BBC's impact and audiences have been proportionately greater than our comparative broadcasting hours would indicate.

Whether a language service is large or small, the pattern of output is similar. All carry a central spine of news bulletins, usually nine minutes long, and read without interruption by despatches or the actuality sound of events. This is the characteristic and distinctive sound of most World Service news broadcasting in whatever language. These bulletins are centrally produced by the Newsroom. The news stories included will take account of varying regional or national interests. But the news bulletin is not, and never has been, adapted in editorial tone or line to fit a particular political situation.

Beyond that, each language service according to its hours and resources carries correspondents' despatches, news analysis, and then broadens its coverage to include arts, science, magazines and human interest subjects. Many of the analyses are also centrally written in order to ensure that there is only one BBC voice in use.

But what was the atmosphere and the society into which these broadcasts were being transmitted? Without understanding the intellectual assumptions of closed communist societies, the role of radio during those years – the 1950s, 1960s and 1970s – long before television could leap frontiers – cannot remotely be understood.

First, all internal media were controlled by the Communist Party. No-one could have a voice on them, or in the written media, without conforming to the Party line. Second, freedom of speech and expression was seen as a bourgeois deception of the masses, adhered to only because it assisted the bourgeoisie themselves in clinging on to power. Third, the media were not designed to spread impartial information but to strengthen the role and power of the Communist Party. Fourth, the Party-controlled media were naturally telling the "objective" truth because they reflected the Party's own "objective" understanding of facts and events. Since the Party was based on Dialectical Materialism, which set out the correct understanding of the way that history was going, it was wise intellectually, as well as prudent politically, to see things the way the Party did. After all "History" was on its side and those who could not see that had to be cured of the errors of their unreconstructed ways of thinking.

It is increasingly difficult as time passes to recapture the full flavour of the dictatorship of the dialectic, or to believe that it could tyrannise whole societies as it did. But a re-reading of George Orwell's *1984*, Arthur Koestler's *Darkness at Noon*, or more recently Anatoli Rybakov's *Children of the Arbat* quickly drags the reader back into a nightmare where black is white if the Party says so, and the majority had no choice but to say it agreed.

In the Communist Bloc, as in the New Testament, truth was most vividly contained in stories. The American journalist, Nicholas Daniloff, tells this definitive Russian joke about thought control:

INTERROGATOR	*Ivan Ivanovich, what do you think of Soviet-American affairs?*
IVAN IVANOVICH	*Well, I think what Pravda writes about it. What Pravda says is what I believe.*
INTERROGATOR	*Ivan Ivanovich, what do you think about relations with China?*
IVAN IVANOVICH	*Well, what Izvestia says about relations with*

	China totally reflects what I believe.
INTERROGATOR	*And what do you think about President Reagan?*
IVAN IVANOVICH	*Well, what Tass put out on its wire yesterday is exactly what I think about President Reagan.*
INTERROGATOR	*Ivan Ivanovich, don't you have any ideas of your own?*
IVAN IVANOVICH	*I do, but I don't agree with them.*

Into such a wholly closed system the foreign radios, among whom BBC World Service was a major player, provided an unwelcome intrusion. For what did they do? They reminded the listener that there was another way of looking at events than the official way; they demonstrated that there was a different way of describing events than the official way; they revealed that there were others besides the listener who could challenge the official line with alternative facts and clinical interpretation. Nicholas Daniloff wrote about the compelling reason for listening:

> Many people used to say to me in Russia that listening to the BBC had developed into something of a habit or an instinct. The need for truthful information was felt almost like a physical need such as hunger or thirst. Time was thought of as either when the BBC was on the air or off. This special sense of time persisted even at moments of great stress, emotional shock or illness. Even when he was being searched or about to be arrested such a person would look at his watch: time to switch on.

This is corroborated by an extraordinary incident which was recorded for us in August 1985:

> On August 19th, 1968, a group of Moscow intellectuals gathered at the flat of one of the dissidents to compile and sign a letter supporting the reforms in Czechoslovakia. The KGB got wind of the gathering and decided to prevent this act of "ideological diversion". Four plain clothesmen and three uniformed militia burst into the flat with a search warrant. At 5.45pm sharp, while the search was still going on, the dissident looked at his watch, turned

*to his friends and said loudly: 'Gentlemen, time for the news, let us
listen to the BBC'. Nobody tried to stop him turning on his radio
set.*

That was the eve of the Soviet-led invasion of Czechoslovakia. By
the time the dissidents returned to their flat after a night in the
police cells, the BBC broadcasts were jammed, a massive state
undertaking which lasted for six years.

Now matching the needs of the audience with the principles of
the broadcaster was not always easy. It was not even universally
agreed that there should only be one BBC World Service voice to
all parts of the world. For many years there was a deep internal
debate about the principles that ought to underlie our broadcasting
to Eastern Europe. It is instructive to read today.

As long ago as 1971, a mere three years after the crushing of the
Prague Spring of 1968, the then Head of the East European
Services, Alexander Lieven examined the question of "Broadcasting to Communist Audiences". He warned of the ingrained
scepticism of an audience who had learned from harsh experience
that all sources of information were to be distrusted. They wanted
accurate news of the outside world; they did not need to be told
that communism was discredited, their daily lives were evidence of
that; so how should we approach listeners so professionally
schooled in their scepticism? Lieven concluded:

> *We should not adopt an automatically hostile attitude, avoid the
> "black and white" approach and, at all costs abstain from
> pettiness, pinpricks, rubbing salt into the wounds, sarcasm,
> polemics or superior "holier than thou" or "you are always wrong"
> attitudes. A cool, detached, almost clinical approach is called for.*

In the same year, as Lieven summed up the departmental consensus
of views on their broadcasting philosophy, that greatest of BBC
commentators on Soviet affairs Anatol Goldberg told a graphic
tale of how not to broadcast to the captive audience – captive, you
might say, but not enslaved:

At the time of the "Spring in Czechoslovakia", a not very experienced colleague was about to introduce a talk on this subject with the remark: 'And now we are going to tell you about events which your press prefers to pass over in silence.' This kind of pinprick would have ruined the talk, since it would have been tantamount to saying that we were giving the information to Soviet listeners only because we knew that it would annoy their Government.

It was therefore specially pleasing for me to receive a letter from the Soviet Union about Goldberg. It came from Andrei Piontkowsky, a scientist and adviser to the powerful opposition group of Soviet Deputies known as the Inter Regional Group. Piontkowsky wrote to me:

The most popular and respected person among Soviet BBC World Service listeners was Anatoli Maksimovich Goldberg. I remember his last prophetic joke in 1982. He was dying when he was told about arrests in Moscow of circus persons connected to Galina Brezhneva, the President's daughter. "Well," said Goldberg, "If the circus is involved, things are really becoming serious."

I should say that this cool, clinical, even dispassionate style had and still has its critics within and without the Soviet Union. The Russian novelist, Andrei Amalryk, complained when he visited the BBC that its output showed what he called "a certain wishy-washiness: on the one hand ... on the other ... I suppose that is how the British are."

No less a giant of Soviet dissidence, Alexander Solzhenitsyn, insisted on visiting the BBC External Services to explain in magisterial terms that this very British approach to events in the Soviet Union was misguided and irrelevant. He indicated that he would be ready to come to Bush House to provide his views on the correct way to broadcast to the Soviet Union. This he did in a ninety-minute monologue, delivered from minutely-written notes on small pieces of checked paper in several colours of ballpoint pen. The essence of it was that the approach of the Anatol Goldbergs of this world was no better than "water trickling through your fingers". On an earlier occasion, Solzhenitsyn had attacked the BBC Russian Service's attempts to improve its radio presentation by declaring memorably "Russia is not for dancing". His conclusion delivered, the great man left. A month later the then Director-General of the BBC, Charles Curran, received a letter from Solzhenitsyn. He explained that he had told Gerard Mansell, then Managing Director of the External Services, what was wrong with the Russian Service only a few weeks ago. Clearly he had done nothing; what was going on?

Solzhenitsyn was looking for a more engaged type of broadcasting, for the approach of a journal de combat. Undoubtedly, some in the World Service thought him right. They did think that totalitarianism should be openly and clearly opposed. They believed that what they saw as plain evil could not be addressed in the same voice as states run on the common or garden variety of simple incompetence, cruelty or selfishness. They did not see the normal BBC rules of detachment or impartiality as relevant in this exceptional historical circumstance. By and large, and over time, the Lieven-Goldberg approach was the one that prevailed, partly because it was accepted as right in its own terms, but also because it was consistent with the rest of World Service broadcasting.

During the Cold War years, we were largely broadcasting in the dark, often in something worse than the dark, in conditions where some of our broadcasts were jammed. The jamming applied to all languages initially but more thoroughly to the Russian and Polish Services. Naturally the Soviet Union was responsible for the jamming of the broadcasts to its own state; less naturally it also took it upon itself to jam the Polish Service into Poland, no doubt as one of the privileges of membership of the Warsaw Pact.

The jamming was disruptive and intrusive as it was intended to be. But it was never total and it was certainly expensive. One BBC estimate put the cost of jamming broadcasts in Russian as some $800 million per year. Even that massive effort was directed to the large towns and cities. It left the rural areas comparatively lightly jammed, and in the process left one window slightly ajar. The jamming did not run through the entire period of the Cold War. But in the case of the Russian Service it was on for long enough – from 1949 to 1963 with a small break in 1956; the invasion of Czechoslovakia in 1968 brought the jammers into operation once again. Lifted in 1973, it was re-imposed in 1980 in the middle of the Polish crisis. It was lifted yet again in January 1987, surely for the last time.

Even jamming attracted that black humour which was the secret weapon of hapless East Europeans in the Cold War. A story circulating in 1982 in Moscow told of a Soviet police-man finding a drunk, lying in the gutter and murmuring. Bending over the man to hear better, the policeman made out the slurred words: "This is the Voice of America". Quick as a flash, the dutiful policeman immediately began to go: "Buzz ... Buzz ... Buzz."

Naturally audience research in the Soviet bloc was impossible, letters scant, and telephone communication rare. Our broadcasters were broadcasting in the dark, taking a massive amount on trust. But from time to time, evidence came through that there was indeed somebody out there. One of the most significant came during the same meeting that I have just described with Alexander Solzhenitsyn. The reason that he thought it worthwhile to tell the BBC what he saw as the correct way to broadcast to the Soviet Union was precisely because he knew that the broadcasts had an impact. A senior BBC journalist in Bush House at the time gave me this account of Solzhenitsyn's comments:

> He opened his remarks by saying that we should not mislead ourselves into thinking that our broadcasts to the Soviet Union were only heard by a small number of malcontents, dissidents and intellectuals. The whole of our broadcasts were monitored and transcribed for the Politburo in full. A substantial digest was distributed to the Central Committee throughout the country. So what we were saying had considerable influence on the way they

reacted to sensitivities. The Soviet authorities were so impressed by the broadcasts that they felt they ought to know what was being said "so they could answer in their propaganda" and to find out what was being heard by their own population.

But trying to blot out the BBC Russian Service was not enough. The most remarkable tribute to their impact came, surely, in 1979. Then, the Soviet Communist party issued a 250-page report on the BBC External Services, designed to arm their party cadres against ideological subversion and called: "Imperialism: The events, facts and documents". It accused us of passing secret messages through the broadcasts to agents in Eastern Europe. It warned against susceptibility to these "highly trained propagandists" who were all the more plausible because of their "reasonable and civilised tone". These so-called "gentlemen" were identified by the Soviet Communist party book as no less "dangerous and insidious" than the more blatant propagandists emanating from Washington or Bonn. The BBC response at the time noted that the entire book was posited on one revealing assumption: that all its official party and governmental recipients knew all about the broadcasts against which they were being warned.

A more recent witness to the impact of our broadcasts is the scientist I mentioned earlier, Andrei Piontkowsky. His story is a remarkable one. I have it both from him, and confirmed by an academic friend in Cambridge, to whom Piontkowsky first spoke. He used to listen mainly to the World Service in English – his English was good enough, the jamming of Russian too obtrusive.

One day in the spring of 1972, he heard one of our science programmes reporting a presentation in London by an American scientist, Dennis Meadows, on his theory about the "Limits to Growth". Such ideas were comparatively novel then, years before today's environmental agenda had formed. Piontkowsky was struck by Meadows' ideas about the global impact of national environmental policies. They were quite new to him. He and a friend took a taxi to the Lenin Library in Moscow, borrowed the book as soon as it was available and smuggled it out of the building. They took it to their university, photocopied it, and smuggled it back into the Lenin Library. Armed with the details of the book, Piontkowsky and his colleagues then began their own work based on the Meadows book and set up the Soviet Group on Global Modelling. In his letter to me Piontkowsky states modestly:

> I think our research and public education in this field in the Soviet Union proved to be very productive in the forming of global consciousness and the so-called "new political thinking" of the Soviet decision-makers. It may be mentioned here that at any rate two of Gorbachev's close advisers – G. Shachnarzarov and I. Frolov – had permanent connections with the Soviet Global Modelling Group.

My academic friend from Cambridge, Dr. Gwyn Prins, who first told me of Piontkowsky's story is more emphatic about the impact of his work.

> The role of Piontkowsky's global modelling work in forming the "New Thinking" cannot be overestimated. He is emphatic that without the World Service, the chain of conversion would have been impossible.

That strikes me as a quite remarkable example of the power of radio communication to spread information, open minds and then alter politics. It does not do that always, but then you might reflect that to do it once in the manner described is enough.

But there is still further first-hand testimony which reveals yet another way in which foreign broadcasts got under the mental skin of a closed society. It came from Oleg Gordievsky, a former KGB colonel, who became a Western double agent, escaped when the KGB became suspicious and has subsequently been advising Western leaders on the best way to understand the nature of, and how to deal with, the Gorbachev team.

Early in 1990, Gordievsky came out in public from his secure hiding place, in a lengthy interview on *Panorama*. Since the hair he wore was a wig, and the beard was false too, it is safe to assume that the seaside house he was filmed in was not his actual house and that since he was shown jogging on the windblown sand of a desolate piece of British coast, that he almost certainly lived in Eaton Square. Not to be outdone, American counter-intelligence produced their own Soviet double agent, Oleg Sheymov, also in a lurid wig, ten days later.

In 1990 Gordievsky wrote three lengthy articles about his experiences in *The Times*. In the first, there was the following revealing passage:

> *KGB officers on foreign language courses traditionally began their English lesson listening to summaries of BBC World Service News. However items containing "anti-Soviet items" were erased before the recording was given to the students.*

This brief statement is worth thinking about. There must have been a great deal of world news left even after the excisions. So the KGB trainees – and the KGB recruited the brightest and the best – were exposed to news about the world presented in a totally different way from any news they would have seen or heard on the official media. What effect could it have on them? Not long after the articles appeared I was able to put this question to Oleg Gordievsky directly; his views on the impact of foreign broadcasting on the Soviet Union are worth setting out in some detail.

First, a piece of near poetry: Gordievsky told me that the four key foreign broadcasters, BBC World Service, Radio Liberty, VOA and Deutsche Welle were known collectively as "The Voices". In March 1953, a young, well ideologically-schooled schoolboy, brought up on the Soviet foundation myths of Stalin as all-wise, all-knowing, and all-powerful, stumbled across one of "The Voices" on his radio and was shattered by what he heard. It was a full account of the crimes Stalin ordered, the assassinations, the camps, the autocracy.

"I was in a feverish state for weeks afterwards," Gordievsksy told me, and as a result, when he went on to further party education, was far readier to look critically at the official line than most of his colleagues. So, like Andrei Piontkowsky, one specific foreign broadcast fundamentally altered his approach to life.

Gordievsky confirmed to me in greater detail than he had set out in his *Times* articles the impact that listening to the BBC World Service in English had on the KGB. For a start, they liked the English accent, and the journalistic approach. KGB students at the Andropov and Dzerzhinsky Institutes had to listen regularly; thereafter, officers in the first and second Directorates of the KGB listened as a matter of professional duty.

I asked Gordievsky how the BBC could have had an impact in the higher political reaches of the Party, since Politburo members are not known for much knowledge of English. This was his reply: "A senior figure like that got his information from four sources; first, from official reports from Ministries; second, from the digest made by his assistant of the daily *Tass* summaries of foreign broadcasts and newspapers; third, from papers submitted by research and academic institutes; and last from his family, and his children listened to the 'Voices'. And perhaps in the evening, he would himself tune into the 'Voices' at his bedside".

By the early 1980s, Gordievsky told me, Soviet citizens no longer bothered to conceal that they listened to the foreign radios. You would hear one youth openly talking about what he had heard to his friend on the Moscow Metro. On a return to Moscow in 1983, Gordievsky recalled walking by a huge block of Moscow flats, the kind with several staircase entrances. There was a group of people clustered at each staircase. Every group was listening to a radio. But each staircase had adopted, he noticed, its own radio station – one was listening to the BBC, the next to Radio Liberty and the next to VOA. Each staircase had become a fan club of a different foreign station.

Gordievsky then added these two thoughts: "At 5.45 in the evening, the average Russian would start drinking; the person with the shortwave radio would tune to a radio station. It was a Happy Hour for intellectuals. They would go to extraordinary lengths to listen in. Some worked out that jamming was less effective in rural areas and would take their holidays there in order to get brief access to a good signal, even rowing a boat out into a small lake to be able to listen in peace. Others found that the BBC Polish Service was less heavily jammed than the Russian Service and learned Polish in order to listen in."

What the BBC taught its listeners was to judge critically, to apply critical questioning to problems. In the end that example had its own impact on people reared on ideological certainties. Gordievsky's conclusion is almost embarrassingly fulsome. "It is impossible to over-estimate the importance of the BBC in the Soviet Union. You were like a university to us."

Ultimately, these extraordinary eye witnesses are saying one simple thing – reality broke in. The foreign broadcasters were the voices of reality, albeit with different emphases in their approach. What our voices did was to keep people sane. A colleague who returned from Czechoslovakia recently would listen to two radios at the same time and have the television tuned on too, in order to get as good a fix – an intellectual compass fix in effect – on events as possible. They assured the listener that there was a world outside which conformed more closely to his experience, reasoning and conscience than to the ideologically determined world of the Party.

A price had to be paid. Any individual or society which says one thing while believing another cannot get off scot–free psychologically and many observers of Eastern Europe recently have spoken of the near schizophrenia that has emerged. For the pretence was a long-standing one. When the Speaker of the Polish Senate, Professor Ziulowski lectured at Cambridge recently, I asked him at what stage in the last forty years had the Polish Communist party lost any claim to legitimacy with the people? He answered without hesitation: "1956 – when the first demonstrations were crushed." Imagine living with a political lie on your lips for a quarter of a century! No wonder they turned to the foreign radios.

Yet it was the breaking-in of economic reality that exposed the lies conclusively. A decade ago, before Armenia became synonymous with earthquake and nationalism, a fictional Radio Armenia was the popular vehicle for anti-regime jokes. One listener asked Radio Armenia: "The Government Radio tell me there is plenty of food available but my refrigerator is empty. What should I do?" Radio Armenia's answer: "Plug your refrigerator into your radio."

By the start of the 1980s, Soviet economists were admitting privately that Soviet statistics were worthless and long years of always officially setting higher targets and always officially meeting them could no longer conceal the fact that the standards of living were among the poorest in Europe and declining. Part of the debate which made the recognition of the internal system of institutionalised distortion possible must have sprung from the opening to the world outside that "The Voices" helped to make possible.

As Eastern Europe has opened up, so has the accompanying sense of desolation. A letter writer from Bucharest in February noted sadly: "Courage we have, but we have inherited little in terms of democracy, honesty, work ethic and fair play". In a sense, the real story of the role of the radios during the last fifty years is still to be told. Yet the evidence is accumulating that the international radios were the "Voices in the Dark" which lightened the darkness of their listeners. No-one could ask for a more moving justification of what they do.

First delivered to the National Museums of Scotland
22 November 1990.

CHAPTER 6

BEFORE & AFTER THE FALL

TWO DIARIES FROM CZECHOSLOVAKIA
1961-1990

IN SEPTEMBER 1961, I visited my relations in Czecho-slovakia with my wife, mother, brother and sister. It was our first visit since 1948. It was almost 30 years before I returned, this time with my wife alone in August 1990. My contrasting impressions are described in extracts from the diaries I kept at the time. For almost half a century, crossing frontiers in Eastern Europe was a traumatic experience. The point of entry provides a crucial first snap shot of the experience that awaits the traveller. Over thirty years, this rule of thumb proved all too accurate.

Monday, September 18, 1961. Large green-jacketed German frontier officials at the Weyden crossing point waved us goodbye - the only vehicles of any kind at the crossing. Round a bend in the road, and only a hundred yards away the Czech frontier post of Rozvadov. No barbed wire at this point, only a handful of guards, armed with machine carbines, and all very, very young. A Belgian was already there, on his way to the Brno Fair, and in the process of losing all his magazines: "This propaganda we do not allow inside the country. It is dirty propaganda". A large sign faced us – "Welcome to Czechoslovakia". Initial formalities were slow but steady; elaborate perusal of passports, carnets, and the green card. Declaration of currency followed – all foreign currency must be declared, and you must bring it all back, except travellers' cheques, presumably to prevent Czechs from hoarding Deutsch Marks or Sterling against a possible escape. Cameras, typewriters, transistors, all are covered by this form. Normally, everything has to be written down in triplicate or quadruplicate (the visa form is in quadruplicate and you may not use carbons). This currency form however which is almost as important in

Czecho as your visa, is not copied at all – you carry the only copy of it yourself, and should you lose it, then no doubt the worst possible construction will be put on the fact.

We move to the cars. I open my boot, disclosing a large green suit bag. We open it, and the customs man – a nice-looking lad – swears gently when he sees it contains eight dresses and two suits. They are, we explain, gifts for our relations. He discovers, in all, ten dresses, three suits, twelve pairs of shoes, two sheets, twenty yards of nylon material, coffee, soup, pharmaceutical drugs – everything they can't get or can't afford. An old (1952) gaberdine suit enrages him, as do four pounds of knitting wool. This must not be let in the country he says. Mother follows him inside the customs house, and then returns saying roughly, "George, bring in that piece of paper with the cameras on it, he wants to write down the wool there as well." We had been there about an hour by then, and this was too much. As Ann and Viccy carried in the wool to have it weighed and registered, they held it up to two of the guards as a joke, to see whose eyes it was going to suit best. A bad mistake. Five minutes later, the Guard commander storms in and shouts at Mother: "Madam, I must warn your daughters against any further acts of provocation; my soldiers understand English, and they heard your daughters say that they were going to photograph the guards being bribed with wool; I warn you against any more acts of provocation of this sort."

What good would it be, I thought as we drove away with our tails between our legs, to explain how the misunderstanding had arisen? The charge of provocation is a difficult one to counter, for they had indeed been provoked, and in their eyes whether there is a good or bad reason matters little when set against the fact that provocation has taken place. The fact of provocation – in this society – cannot be mitigated by any explanation of its cause.

Thursday, July 26, 1990. *Thirty minutes out of Hamburg, the border crossing to the former GDR. Deserted, but the demolition men are in already. Piles of twisted metal, and bulldozers and excavators attacking the customs sheds. It was a large crossing point, bigger even than the Marienborn-Helmstedt crossing, and its utter emptiness except for the breakers is good for the soul to behold. The Autobahn is mainly peopled with a steady line of Trabis and the occasional Wartburg, many laden with shopping, some with a single consumer item, others packed with various cardboard boxes. We break every rule in the book and sweep along at 150 kms, thus committing a new sin, that of techno-arrogance. Since they are all slow, all steady and seldom pull out to overtake, it is remarkably safe.*

The GDR is wide, empty, cultivated but curiously inert. It is tempting to read a mood into it – but mistaken. Beyond the Berlin Ring we find evidence of autobahn archaeology – Rasthöfe (motorway cafes) which have not been touched for sixty years; the slip roads to parking sites or to exits are narrow, brief and abrupt; this was all that was needed when they were built to cope with existing car speeds. Now they verge on the dangerous even in a road system fit for Trabis.

Tuesday, July 31, 1990. So to Czecho across the hills from Dresden, welcome and cool. Border crossing only slightly difficult – merely slow. Try my Czech in the bank and it does its work. In many respects a very satisfying border. At one geographical moment on the map they are speaking German. At the next, they are speaking and looking Czech. Annie says: "Isn't it incredible that there seems to have been no Czech woman who ever leapt across the border to cross-breed with a German". But they did not. Every Czech face peering out of the customs post is a Czech.

Hot drive to Teplice. Very dirty and depressed. All heads turn as we park. Two women immediately accost us in German asking to change money. We say no.

*Monday, 18 September, 1961.*We had misjudged the distance badly. Rozvadov to Bystrice was nearly 300 miles, and we only managed half the distance by nightfall. Everything seemed very strange. Petrol stations were hard to find – certainly there were none on the open road – and none of the towns we passed through looked as though they had pubs or restaurants open.

Two of the largest towns were garrison towns with great barrack blocks on their outskirts, and such traffic as there was was mainly military. As we approached Brno, the traffic grew heavier, chiefly buses and heavy lorries, whose exhausts threw out so much black smoke that it was impossible to see oncoming vehicles. After losing one another in Brno and miraculously meeting again almost before we realised we were lost, we decided to stop at the house of some relations in Roussinov for a short rest and something to eat. Here we discovered a major chink in the country's propaganda defences. Anyone can see a non-communist news bulletin by switching his tv set to the Viennese channel. But one wonders what the standard of Austrian tv is?

Hardly was the initial surprise and greetings over when the buzzer rang and my Godmother answered the loudspeaker to the front door downstairs. It was the police. So soon, I thought? It turned out, however, that they were only making sure that the cars were locked. Even, it appears, if you drive an open sports car, you must lock the door when it is parked.

The drive to Bystrice seemed endless. George and I nearly fell asleep at the wheel; I took my shoes off, but it had no effect at all, and only Mother's determination got us to Bystrice by 12.30. Naturally no-one was awake, having decided long since that we couldn't arrive that night; after throwing pebbles at Deda's window, there appeared, after a pause of a few minutes, a comic, bent figure, incredulous at our arrival, and wearing long woollen underpants, a blazer, and a cap.

Tuesday, 19 September, 1961. I had a nightmare in which I dreamed I was in Czechoslovakia. It was in fact less frightening than the drive itself, for we had been convinced that any car that didn't overtake us immediately was deliberately following us. Even though the sound that woke us was a fanfare on the communal loudspeakers to prepare for a Communist Party announcement, a sunny day soon reconciled me to the reality. I'd forgotten what a lovely part of the country Bystrice was in. Hills covered with pine forests on two sides, and lower hills close on the other two. Those on the south and west – they include Hostyn – are surprisingly high, and certainly much higher than I had remembered. Hostyn must be over two and a half thousand feet, and the large shrine church stands out clearly at the top. Most of this however, was hidden in a heavy autumnal heat haze, as thick as a mist.

Saturday, 4 August, 1990.To Bystrice. Very hot and sapping. Motorway runs out soon after Brno. Then longish, pretty country roads through Kromeriz, Huelin, Holesov – the Proustian names of my childhood. Why did nobody tell me that Holesov had a rather fine looking baroque church, still less a synagogue? Why did I not know that these places were a mere few kilometres apart instead of years apart, set in my child's eye in a hierarchy of size and importance dictated by their place in the railway system? If you changed at Prerov for Huelin, and then changed at Huelin for Holesov and Bystrice, this progression of branch lines indicated the diminishing importance and sizes of the towns concerned. In fact the differences are not so big, and the undiscriminating eyes of adults never conveyed to me that these were places with architectural importance – or at least interest – and value in their own right.

How could I not see that Hostyn was on a comparatively high hill – running along a charming series of wooded foothills for miles? Hostyn always seemed insignificant – perhaps by comparison with the Alps? Today they are a major feature of the landscape, unspoiled, running for some miles in a characterful spine. Bystrice itself – recognisable in the sense that the roads lead naturally in the directions that I remembered. The church, the main shopping parade, with Joe Zrubek, the icecream and cake shop, now dismally transmogrified into a state Cukrarna. Hotel Pod Horan is clean, decent and basic. They did not get our reservation but they have a room overlooking the "atrium" – God help us – in fact the yard in which the older men drink their beer. Yet, it is all at once strange and deeply familiar.

[In 1961, all our relatives were still recovering from the impact of the Communinst revolution. They were still coming to terms with a brutal decade.]

Thursday, 21 September, 1961. Our cousin Luba walked us round the town. He has had a hard life. Trained as a vet, he has worked with horses, and latterly at a big stud farm near Prague. The work was hard and the hours long – but you can say that of every job in Czecho today. About five years ago, he was made responsible for buying some stallions for the stud, and soon after he had done so, they became diseased and had to be shot. He was promptly accused of attempting to sabotage the entire stud, and was put up for trial.

There must have been some personal malice behind it somewhere because when he was acquitted by a local court, the case was moved to Prague – Luba remaining under arrest – where a higher court condemned him to four years in the uranium mines. This he survived, to everyone's surprise, though in one period of eighteen months he only saw daylight twice. He came out, if anything, stronger and fitter than when he went in; the authorities are said to be very scrupulous about preventing possible radiation sickness. He was also unbroken and surprisingly unbitter. He might well have felt a comprehensive grudge against everything as his wife hadn't managed to stand the strain of four years absence, and had eloped.

Despite having served a political sentence, he got back his job at the stud. This might suggest that victimisation is a thing of the past, but he soon found out that it would be very difficult for him to get a driving licence, and that travel abroad, even to other Iron Curtain countries, was out of the question for him. (After eighteen months he is still waiting for a driving licence, but they say that he will probably get it soon.) Then came his worst piece of luck. A horse bit his left hand, across the wrist, so badly that the first surgeon who saw it wanted to amputate. Luckily another doctor disagreed, and so began the long process of getting the nerves and the severed muscles to work again. He asked to have a clerical job at the stud until he could handle a horse once more, but – and this is where it seems like victimisation again – this was refused. He must go and work in the collectives until fit, and then he can try and get his job back again.

Saturday, 23 September, 1961. Alenka's husband, Jarda, came home today, and Luba and I went to collect him from the nearest main line station. He works at Ostrava all week, and returns home at weekends only. A big, lean, good looking man, he is a motor mechanic, devoting his working time to servicing heavy plant, and his spare time to tuning racing bikes.

He and Alenka must live a curious life. There are two constants in it – mathematical constants, as it were: (a) they can't get a house near Ostrava, (b) Alenka needs to work, and someone must look after the children while she does. The solution is for them to occupy two rooms in Bobina's house; Bobina looks after the children, Alenka works at Bystrice as a radiographer, and Jarda commutes to Ostrava. The one good result is that they earn a lot of money; she has about £75 a month, and he about £100, but he earns every penny of it, working an average of 300 hours a month, on a five-day week.

This incidentally is one of the secrets of the system. How do you exhaust the nation so that it has no time for plotting and discontent? The answer is that everyone works very long hours and starts work very early. As far as I can see, everyone is at work by 6.30 in the morning, and so thinks in terms of going to bed at 9 at night. The evenings hardly exist, and social life doesn't exist either. Such leisure time as people have is provided for by the TV. The nation is too exhausted even to think of rebellion. In Jarda's case you can see why. He must work nearly fifteen hours a day, which forces him to be on the job from six in the morning to nine at night. His resentment of the system comes out when he gets drunk, but normally he is too tired to do anything else but sleep.

Alenka works in a slightly different way. As a radiographer, she has to visit people in the district round Bystrice, and these visits total about thirty a month. Now she is given no transport to do the travelling efficiently – she can cycle if it's close, or take a bus. However she travels, she may then find that the person she's gone to see is out, and the time is wasted. But how she fits in her quota of visits with her other work is for her to resolve.

Sunday, 5 August, 1991. *The message from our Czech relatives was that of course, the revolution was wonderful but a lot needed to be done. Jarda spoke most. Until people take independence into their own economic hands, nothing will have been achieved. Everyone is so used to being told what to do that they will wait to be told. At Rusava, a lovely spot nestling in the Hostynske Vrchy (Hills), we wanted a soft drink at 5 pm on a hot Sunday. The restaurant was closed because that was the regulation. The waiters had no incentive to work on or to increase takings or give service. They filled their plan and that was their only duty. What is so extraordinary is that so few people have taken matters into their own hands and struck out for independence. At Rusava too, there is a Farmers' Union hotel with a glorious view down an unspoiled wooded, hilly valley. Why did not somebody take it over and turn it into a hotel? Jarda said that while the idea was that this should happen, there were so many rules and regulations that it was not happening. And of course they need foreign investment. But the investors will only come in if they can get a 30-50% rate of return and that they can't yet see. So there is a blank stagnation around.*

Prices are abjectly low by our standards. We get 44 crowns to the pound, and at this rate, most meals cost £1 per head. With beer. Dinner with wine could run up to £3 per head. The dinner at the Forum in Prague was going it at £12 each. A bottle of wine in a supermarket costs 50p. Yet these are real rates for Czechs. When they have to pay the premium on foreign currency to go abroad – they should be so lucky – it puts foreign travel to a Europe which is now theoretically open to them, beyond their day to day reach. The gap in purchasing power between us and them is embarrassing. How to avoid playing the American Uncle, the rich cousins, the members of a successful society so that it does not humiliatingly rub in not only that they have been messed around by a corrupt political society, but left impoverished too? Yet there is no lack of dignity, no self pity, no envy, no lack of realism about the future on their part.

*Thursday, 21 September, 1961.*Most evenings Bobina, Luba and Alenka come round after supper and we all sit round the table with beer, wine or in Deda's case, slivovice. He brews it himself from the best selected plums, and it has a taste like no other slivovice or schnapps I have ever had – a pure sweet warmth that moves from the stomach outwards, seemingly unintoxicating and very stimulating. Deda usually starts the day with a glass or two, and then cycles off to the orchard with a hip-flask full. He needs it too, for at the height of the season he works hard, even climbing trees to shake the loose fruit down. Then he picks or gathers it, loads it into baskets, swings a basket onto each handlebar and cycles back home. He claims to have carried 800 kgs in this way last year.

There is a big war panic on at the moment. Besides the mobilisation, which appears to be large, there has been a run on the shops for two basic goods: salt and vinegar. Salt of course is the time-old reaction of the poor in a war emergency – buy salt to preserve your food for a long time. This is certainly one of the reasons behind the demand, but the other is more significant still; it has been said that salt and vinegar are a good cure for radiation and flash burns! On top of this, Bobina's Communist husband, Manta – a Communist for reasons of comfort rather than principle – returned from a party meeting to say that plans were in hand for the evacuation to Russia of all children under 13 in the event of nuclear war.

This is just one of the many signs that make Czechs convinced that the Russian hand sits harder on Czecho than perhaps anyone in the West would care to admit. They all asked us: "When will the Russians go? Will it be long?" Deda has sworn that he will see the present regime out, and at 84 he looks good for another six years. But the young feel more hopeless; to them six years is a large chunk out of their best years, and they can't sit and wait. Luba complained bitterly that Zapotocky once said: "We want to restrain nobody – if you disagree, then leave." Now of course this is a mockery; even the Communists, it seems, had their naive periods. Escaping is dangerous and difficult, and the mind turns to the other alternatives – a political miracle. "How long" said Luba, "will it be? two years, four years?" I couldn't pretend certainty where I knew there was none, and I said that if there were changes in ten years time, this would in any case depend on an internal movement in Czecho, as there had been in Hungary and Poland. When Luba heard this, he went out and wept.

[My cousin, Luba, did not live to see the end of Communist rule. He died of leukaemia in 1975.]

Tuesday, 7 August, 1990. *Nice drive to Zlin over the Hostynske Vrchy, very unspoiled landscape, fully wooded, mainly conifer but often breaking into hardwoods – and the occasional farm and settlement in a clearing reminding you of civilisation. Zlin – the "Bata" company town – is a very different kettle of fish. Large-ish and industrial, with the "other side" of the valley from the original company town utterly covered with a "new town" of flats and tower blocks. We ask for the Hotel Slovakia. No-one has heard of it. We look at the Cedok voucher – it is for a hotel in Zilin in Slovakia! Fortunately the "Moskva", formerly Spolecensky Dum, has a room.*

Look at the Department store, formerly Obchodni Dum, and are shocked by its deep poverty, the limitation of its goods, the cheapness of its toys, the poverty of the basic materials and the derisory sums they cost to us, thus advertising the difference between the two standards of living. My half-uncle Ruda comes to fetch us. Our original family house has been lovingly protected, and is a good, roomy, handsome 30's house. Two highspots to the evening. I ask them what they think of Havel: Dobra, Ruda's wife replies, "Marvellous, such a moral man". What do they want of the revolution? Their adopted son, a builder called Peter: "Freedom! To do what I want, when I want, how I want". It was a marvellously cheering moment. How long will he wait for things to get better? Five years, but not much more. But then which of us can think beyond five years? More relative costs. Ruda earns Kcs 16 per hour as a calculator repair man. Peter thinks that Kcs 25 for the Hotel Moskva disco is a lot. We work out very roughly that the differential between the two standards of living is anything up to eight times.

Monday, 25 September, 1961.This evening Jozka informed us that we couldn't have any beer with supper as the entire town had been without beer since Saturday afternoon. Private enterprise has its faults, but... Mention of shortages reminds me of others. Pencils are difficult to get, as are good hand towels. Clothing is of course a major difficulty as a suit costs more than most people's monthly salary, and to have a pair of shoes soled costs about 30/–. What the family would do without Mother's clothes parcels I can't think; Viccy's dresses appear on Lydia and Alenka, our shirts on Jan and Mirek; Deda's proudest possession is a double breasted, dark blue, gold-buttoned blazer! Without these they would be in rags.

Such are the contradictions of a communised society: an agricultural area where meat is short, and milk and potatoes in uncertain supply; a highly forested area where wood is almost impossible to get; a country which prides itself on its beer and runs short of it. These are the superficial signs of the deeper contradictions; the society is short of labour, but directs its labour force on ideological rather than on economic grounds; the society offers an educational system based on ability, but appoints to jobs according to political consideration; as a materialistic way of life it fails; and as a metaphysical expression of an ideal way of life it fails to enlist support or even sympathy.

Thursday, 9 April, 1990. *Overcast but still gets hot by midday. Fine, open country from Telc to Jindrichuv Hradec, good but busy square, some fine houses including one which is well painted. Walk right round castle, big, commanding, elaborate, but in an appalling state of disrepair, though some restoration is underway. By now the overall dilapidation is beginning to get us down. It is not just that most places are dirty, but most of the town houses are showing the signs of fifty years of neglect. It is appalling and will take a generation to put right. It is as if the CP decided that they would put money into new "workers' flats" – much easier to control socially and politically – and put nothing into the old town centres. They were not pulled down or actually destroyed but no-one lifted a little finger to keep them standing. After a while – by this Thursday to be exact – the dilapidation was well past the stage that any visitor or traveller might think of as merely picturesque.*

Lunch at Trebon, another walled town with a simple town square, many surprise houses and an over-restored parish church. Carp for lunch – bony and sticky, inconvenient fish. Though beer still good, it is beginning to be an insufficient reason to enjoy otherwise impoverished meals. On holiday, food matters! Countryside and pretty towns are beginning to pall in the persistent heat and the drain of constant difficulties. Cesky Krumlov is a pretty, tortuous, river-encircled town, with narrow streets and a fine tall castle on a crag. Buildings again are generally very dilapidated, although the main square is in a reasonable condition – but actually less attractive than Jindrichuv Hradec.

Hotel up an inaccessible one way street but it looks fairly new, and the room is nice – overlooking a great sweep of the Vltava. First pull of the lavatory cord pulls it off – it is only thin string. I drive off to park, and inadvertently drive up a poorly signed, quiet one-way street the wrong way. Half way up it, I am aware of a red

95

Lada driving up to me, hooting frantically, almost running into me. I let it pass and wonder whether to go past it at the cross roads. Out storms a young policeman, shouting in German "Get out of the car, turn it off, where are your papers, why are you driving without it, this is a one way street!" I tell him to speak English, avoid threatening behaviour, do not refuse to obey him, but agree to go back to the hotel for my papers. I explain to Annie what has happened, slowly go upstairs, slowly get my driving licence, and then pay the Kcs 500 fine. He has now calmed down. But they do teach them to behave like bullies. That is how they treat people. Irony – as we chatted yesterday about our unspendable Kcs, Annie suggested committing our favourite traffic offence and then paying the fine for it. Slightly chilling to have a wish come so true so quickly.

*Tuesday, 26 September, 1961.*It was initially a relief to get to Prague, to see busy streets, full shops, and a comparative air of normality. It didn't take long to destroy this mood. We found a restaurant on the Vaclavske Namesti which turned out to be pretty filthy. The food, as usual in present day Czecho, was measured by the gramme, and 100 grammes is not much – but all shares are equal and must seen to be equal. We asked for beer. "Sorry, no beer". Pause. "Are there licensing hours then?" "No, but if we served beer after 3 o'clock, we wouldn't have any for the evening".

After the normal bureaucratic struggle at Cedok – the state travel agency – we got a hotel and walked there, leaving the cars where they were. At the hotel the receptionist refused to let us into the rooms until we had showed our passports – leaving us in no doubt that the whole hotel business is a branch of the police – and then a policeman proved to be extremely difficult about letting us park in front of the hotel. As a crowd gathered too quickly for our liking we gave in and moved on.

A black market restaurant provided us with good food in the evening – no nonsense about weighing the food there. On the way back to the hotel, we stopped in front of a man's hat shop that particularly attracted our attention, for it was full of those broad-brimmed trilbies beloved of Central European politicians especially when worn with an ankle length, fur lined, double breasted, large-buttoned greatcoat. They're a funny sight and we had mild hysterics over them – we had, after all, to laugh at something – but we soon stopped as a small, puzzled crowd gathered around us. I decided I wanted to leave Prague pretty soon, and George agreed with me.

* * *

Both trips ended in a bad atmosphere. On September 27, early in the morning, my Uncle Jozka left the Hotel Europa in Vaclavske Namesti to post a letter. On his return, the concierge would not allow him back into his room "because he was not staying there". After breakfast, as my wife and I were returning up the stairs to our room, the same concierge stormed out from behind his desk shouting "That woman is not staying in this hotel, she must not go upstairs." It took a furious shouting match between him and me and my brother before we faced him down. We packed, and drove to the border, jumping at shadows. At Rozvadov, the border guard who had so insistently itemised those gifts that we must not leave inside Czechoslovakia, spotted us and cycled down from his quarters to supervise our exit personally. In 1990, we saw a waiter standing at the entrance of the cafe at the same Hotel Europa turning people away in the great continuing traditions of socialist service.

In August 1990, the incident with the policeman had unsettled us. Besides the food situation was getting us down. We could not rely on getting dinner anywhere in Cesky Krumlov; in the morning, the cafe in the square served cake and not bread because it was not licensed to sell bread. Food is a matter of politics – in the Soviet Union, the restaurant menus were like the Soviet Constitution; perfect, complete and comprehensive on paper. In practice, most items – like freedom, or beef – were permanently off. The failure of the Czechoslovak Communists to organise food distribution – or rather, their well-nigh total success in preventing adequate food distribution in a country fat with it – was a reflection of the rest of their failure. As we stood outside the Monastery of Vyssi Brod in Southern Bohemia with the sun glinting off Smetana's beloved Bohemian woods and fields, and the ripples of the delicious Vltava, I said to Ann: "If we pack now and drive like hell we can have dinner in Germany." "Those are the most beautiful words you have ever uttered." We packed, we drove, we did eat in Germany. The relief was indescribable.

CHAPTER 7
TRADITORE, TRADUTTORE
CAN MANY LANGUAGES REALLY SPEAK WITH ONE VOICE?

I T SEEMED to me one of the most challenging ideas that I ever learned: that the translation of an original might fundament- ally betray the intended meaning of the author. It seemed shocking and slightly pleasurable too; given that so few readers would know the original, what room there was for the translator to take liberties?

Over the years, the question of translations and their value has taken on an even greater significance. How does one know that David Magarshack is a better translator of Dostoevsky than Constance Garnett? More fluent perhaps, more idiomatic – in the style of the 50s at least – but better? Whom do you trust over Proust? Scott-Moncrieff or Terence Kilmartin? Is it a matter of trust, or the creation of an equivalent verbal idiom to the original? Or is it ease of reading, even of sheer laziness? Do you like your *Tale of Genji* in Arthur Waley's rendering or in Seidensticker's? Why is it that some translations read like translations – conveying a sense of careful, over literal versioning rather than imaginative equivalence? And finally, in the absence of knowledge of the orig- inal, are such impressions worth the paper they are written upon?

I had no doubts about the difficulties of translation before I reached Bush House. In the last five years, I have learned enough about the nature and structure of languages other than English to make me even more respectful of those who have to take the picturesque, wayward, over-endowed, generous tongue that is English and turn its often hazy meanings into the tongues that millions of other people understand.

The World Service broadcasts in 38 languages. In typically chauvinistic English manner, the official Bush House rubric usually refers to our broadcasts in "English and 37 other languages", as if implying that English is some kind of meta-language in a category of its own. The most difficult question that any Managing Director can be asked is: "How do you know what the other languages are saying?" The World Service defines itself as talking "with one voice but in many languages", but who is responsible for ensuring that such a noble claim is true? I was, and still am, asked these questions frequently. At the outset, the only honest answer that I could give to both those questions was "I don't", and "Not me", respectively.

In 1986, we set out to remedy both defects in a modest way, by setting up an occasional, systematic, centrally supervised method for looking into the way the 37 languages went about their task of translating the news and analytical material which forms an important core of their broadcasting output. In doing so, we set out on a Long March through the deserts and swamps of interpretation, grammar, syntax, nuance, accuracy and equivalence that represent the dangerous territory which any translator must cross when he tries to move from one language to another and from which many never return to tell any tale with conviction. In the process, we learned a great deal about the languages in which this broadcasting Tower of Babel communicates, but still more about the language with which they all – because they broadcast from London – must start.

Back in 1986, the process of recording the output of three days of broadcasting of a language service without prior warning, having it translated back into English outside the BBC, comparing the back-translation with the original from which much of it came, noting the discrepancies or errors, and finally reviewing the results with a group of a dozen broadcasters from all over the World Service, was considered at once editorially novel, personally threatening, and culturally offensive by some. Nevertheless, it was begun, despite protests, and the starting point was Hausa, an important West African language, spoken by 61.5 million people in the North of Nigeria and by a further 4.5 million in a broad belt to the East. The BBC Hausa Service enjoys a large following and commands an audience of around 8 million. Hausa seemed as good a place as any to start.

Any idea that comparing translations would be a simple matter of accuracy – either it was right or it was wrong – fell at the first fence. The Hausa Service Head began his note on the language with the masterful observation: "As in life itself, two of the greatest problems for translators from English into Hausa are sex and the family". That was throwing down the gauntlet with a vengeance – a sentence, by the way, virtually untranslatable into any other language. If all language is indeed dead metaphor, then English appears to relish the corpses more than most. But why do the Hausa have difficulty with sex, linguistically at least? For a start, they need to know the gender of a correspondent before completing the sentence. The common phrase, "A correspondent sent us this despatch" leaves the Hausa translator frozen into in- action. He – or she – cannot begin the sentence without knowing if the correspondent is male or female.

The Hausa Service office is filled with the sounds of queries such as "Is Hilary a man or a woman? Or Francis? Or Robin?" For all I know, millions of Hausa labour under the illusion that the BBC's UN correspondent Chris Gunness is a woman. Once you move into family matters in Hausa land, things become even more complex. To refer to the "President's brother or sister" is hopelessly imprecise. "Is he the younger brother or the older brother? This is a crucial social distinction and each relation has a distinct single word to reflect this. So too with sisters. And aunts and uncles must be either maternal or paternal – again each has its separate single word in Hausa. And cousins, nieces and nephews have no immed- iate one-word equivalents in Hausa. The exact relationship has to be specified: son of one's mother's younger brother, daughter of one's elder sister, etc".

Things do get better after marriage, the Hausa Service went on, beginning to enjoy itself: "there are no translation problems with the in-laws. Vagueness is the rule rather than specificity: any male relation by marriage is 'suruki' and any female relation by marriage is 'suruka'. This usually includes all blood-relations of your spouse and all blood-relations of all spouses of your own blood-relations! Anyone who falls into this usually vast group is covered by this one word (with its masculine or feminine form) and is usually referred to as such without further specification. The problem for translators is rendering 'suruki' or 'suruka' into English!"

Next, we took on Polish. The Poles are proud people, and a

much listened to Service. In their note on translation, a senior member of the Service set out to explain with as much simplicity and subtlety he could muster that English was a crude, clodhopping tongue, unsuited to conveying the simple things of life. He took the seemingly innocuous phrase, used a thousand times a day at Bush House in introducing items in news programmes, "James Smith of the BBC explains..." The point is not how to translate the Polish back into English but how to get it into Polish accurately in the first place. It is a phrase which – he observed – has caused "untold differences" in the Service, generating "heated linguistic controversies over cultural differences between Britain and Poland" and much else besides. (The picture this reveals of daily routine in the Polish Service is intriguing.) Why does this phrase cause such difficulties?

"We couldn't say simply 'of the BBC' because in Polish it some-how implied a distance. It conveyed the idea of us being located away from the BBC and of merely summoning James Smith to our microphones together with a string of other people. And that wouldn't do, of course."

The difficulty was that the phrase "of the BBC" was so obvious and banal that Polish listeners did not give, according to the Polish Service, "two hoots in a hollow whether James Smith was on the payroll of the BBC or the London School of Political Wisdom". Next, the Poles tried and rejected a phrase such as "James Smith, a BBC *employee*." "That carried most unfortunate class distinctions, implying that James Smith was not really one of us. In Polish, *employee* sounds almost as disparagingly neutral as that nasty English expression 'our friend here says'...".

They moved on to "James Smith, a BBC commentator", fine in Polish but seriously adrift from BBC journalistic orthodoxy.

"The BBC emphatically did not comment on anything. It confined itself to facts, accompanied on occasion by modestly boring fact analysis. To call anybody a BBC commentator was a serious offence fraught with serious consequences".

In the end, they told me, the Polish Service settled for "BBC collaborator". It was not lowly like *employee*, or politically dubious like *commentator*. It was – as they put it – a phrase of genteel grandeur befitting the high moral tone of the BBC as purveyor of unadulterated truth. In English, of course, it would almost be insulting but in Polish: "A BBC *collaborator* implied someone who, like an English gentleman and a scholar, doesn't have to do this for a living, you know; someone who drops by and shares his precious wisdom with us; someone who, because of his independent means (a hint of the old nobility) is to be implicitly trusted; someone who, being an avuncular figure, is at the same time possessed of high moral qualities and acceptable social background."

The Polish Service concluded their morally improving tale which should have been called "What's in a Word", with the following observation: "Firstly, that there is more to cultural diversity than meets the eye, and secondly, that translations are like women: if they are beautiful, they aren't faithful; if they're faithful, they aren't beautiful".

It was the Russian Service which first put into precise words for me the sheer scale of the undertaking of translating factual news into another language under the pressure of deadlines and within specifically timed programme slots. It seemed an almost impossibly heroic undertaking. (Of course, it is very Russian to present any activity or job, however routine, as a heroic undertaking, but let that pass.) With admirable economy, the Senior Producer in the Russian Service provided this scholarly warning: "English is an analytical language, i.e. relationship between words is expressed through word order or syntax. It is dominated by syntax to such an extent that an adequate translation sometimes requires total transformation of the sentence. It should be remembered that fixed word order in English brings the semantic centre of gravity forward in the sentence, while in Russian the tendency is opposite. Particular attention should be paid to adverbial modifiers of time and place with which a Russian sentence normally begins. Lazy translators slavishly follow the word order of the original."

With our attention now thoroughly alerted to differences in word order in different languages, some startling instances were drawn to our attention. The BBC Burmese Service broadcasts for seven and a half hours a week. It is widely regarded as the only reliable source of information that the Burmese people have, living as they do under a particularly repressive regime. Probably millions of Burmese listen. The Head of the Service noted "Translation to

Burmese scrambles English word order. In Burmese, adjectives and prepositions follow nouns, but subordinate clauses precede. The verb goes right at the end. So the English order is changed, both between chunks in a sentence and within each chunk. This splits up words which started off together, and if the sentence is long it becomes more difficult to know what links up with what."

He then obligingly provided some examples. Take a very simple news story in English: "Members of the Lebanese Parliament have resumed their meeting in the Saudi Arabian town of Taif to try to agree on political reforms to bolster the present ceasefire in Lebanon". You see what the Russian Service means when they pointed out that the semantic centre of gravity lies forward in an English sentence. In Burmese word and sense order, the reverse is true. That sentence would become in Burmese: "Lebanon within, present ceasefire bolster in-order-to, political reforms try agreement concerning, Saudi Arabia country Taif town within, Lebanon parliament members meeting again convened."

Burmese is not alone in conveying meaning in this way. The Head of the Turkish Service declared flatly: "Syntax is totally different from and incompatible with English". He too gave an example. The following sentence: "Iranian forces at the southern front are reported to have captured the town of Eternia, following their renewed attacks on Iraqi territory," would become: "Southern front at the, Iranian forces, on Iraqi territory renewed attacks following, Eternia town captured are reported." By way of a throw-away remark, he added: "There is no verb 'to have', nor are there any relative pronouns".

Now you can get used to the idea that syntax is differently arranged without too much difficulty even if you have never learned another language. After all, why shouldn't the meaning of a sentence be driven from the end, once you have all the rest of the information before you? But it was the sheer scale of difference of other languages that became more acute the longer we probed into the way they translated.

The depth of the difference was first dramatically highlighted by the Turkish Service Head: "Verbs are somewhat different in Turkish usage, e.g., 'gidiyor' may mean: is going, will go, is on his way, goes or is about to go, depending on context. There is no distinction between present and past participles."

Yet this was as nothing compared to Finnish. Its Head observed cheerily that since it is not an Indo-European language it is a pretty odd bird in Europe. She then admitted what few of us want to confront – that Finnish thought processes – not merely word order, please note – are significantly different from their European neighbours. We are not handling verbal jigsaws: the world looks different in a different tongue. She then set out the following killing list of comments on the sheer particularity of Finnish: "It is a very down-to-earth language, with a maddening shortage of abstract nouns. There is no definite or indefinite article. There is only one personal pronoun doing duty for both 'he' and 'she'.Nouns have fifteen declensions, of which some thirteen are currently used. Some nouns can on occasion be used in a comparative or superlative mode, like adjectives. Verbs have four infinitives, some of which can be declined as nouns! Present tense has to cover also future, continuous, intended or habitual action."

Faced with such a catalogue of deeply structural differences it was a comparative relief to turn to the simplicity of an East Asian language such as Vietnamese, even if it lacks verbs with tenses or passive or subjunctive moods. Even this warning about the subtlety of the Vietnamese language was comparatively easy to absorb: "Most abstract concepts are expressed by two words with their own individual meaning which, just like sweet and sour sauce, combine to become something totally different from the original ingredients – although not all Vietnamese would agree about what the final product really is."

In the case of Somali, we have a special responsibility. The language had no written form until 1972. It is a Cushitic language, much enriched by its links with Arabic through 800 years of Islam. Yet Arabic was not thought fit to be the orthographic form for Somali because, as the language of the Holy Koran, it was too sacred to be sullied with ordinary Somali sounds. A unique Somali script was devised but rejected on the understandable grounds that it would have given too much standing to the particular clan to which the originator belonged.

It took a decision by a Socialist dictator, Siad Barre, aided by UNESCO, to adopt the Roman script of the former colonial powers – Italy, France and Britain. The broadcasts of our Somali Service where translation often takes place live, verbatim at the microphone, are an important ingredient in the development of the language. Our broadcasts not only convey information – they are actually forming the language. In writing about the problems this brings, the Somali Service Head noted somewhat cryptically:

".. equally important is a noble poetic heritage with its uniquely competitive poetry. That poetry is an invaluable archive but it is also a debating chamber and even a jousting arena."

In this atmosphere, the peculiarities of the Thai language threw up something wholly new for us – not word order, not the nature of verbs, but a class consciousness to make even the English blench, with different words being used by different social classes: "For instance the Royal Family *deigns to put food to their mouths* whereas the common people *scoff rice*. In the Section we tend to use middle-class Thai such as *sacrifice one's life* instead of the more common word for die. This is a subject of continuing discussion and sometimes controversy within the Section. But when referring to Royals, whether Thai or foreign, we know we are expected to use a special language or otherwise be accused of *lèse-majesté*. For this we have a special dictionary and it is sometimes difficult to use. For example on one occasion we had difficulty in determining the Royal word for flu. In any case Royal language takes twice as long in air time than everyday Thai."

Despite these huge differences in the very nature of the different kinds of sound that we call language, the overwhelming message from the evaluations of the language services was reassuring. There were some weak translators, but some sections were outstandingly good, accurate and indeed imaginative in transferring English idiom to their own. We came across no instance where meaning had been deliberately distorted for political reasons. Numbers often caused problems – particularly in Hindi or Mandarin where rendering of western numbers into theirs can take many seconds, thumb-sucking and speculation even during a conversation.

As the process continued, we suddenly realised that what we were evaluating was not the "other" languages, but English itself. It was the Finnish Service Head who made this exact admonition about the habitual vagueness of English:

"Precision is the key word, especially in news and current affairs type of language. Expressions such as *earlier, for a short while* are far too vague for a Finn. *An official* can be anything from a lowly clerk to a senior civil servant. 'A man has been arrested in France. He is...' just cannot be translated word for word; Finns need some definition to *man* in the first sentence, e.g. 'Thirty-year-old house-painter Gaston Duval has been arrested....' Cities, buildings etc. are not personified in Finnish. Thus, *Pentagon* must be translated as 'the Ministry of Defence of the United States', and *Bonn* as 'the Government of the Federal Republic of Germany', if that is what is meant."

The Finns were pointing the finger directly but only implicitly at the main characteristic of English, its shiftiness. Time and time again during these lengthy sessions, our foreign language colleagues would complain about the plethora of weasel words in English. It is littered with implications, inferences, innuendoes, with deliberate imprecision. References to time are vague; references to quantity are imprecise; actual accusations are turned into something oblique. Hints of meaning masquerade as statements of fact. The English language emerged as misty as its landscape, the emanation of a people who had created a language perfectly adapted to suit their own refusal to say what they mean. It was left to the Hungarians – those distant linguistic cousins of the Finns – to confront this basic characteristic of English in plain words. The elegant exposé of the nature of English by a Hungarian colleague is magisterial:

"As for the peculiarity of English, most difficulties arise from the sophistication of English in glossing over missing or unwanted information and in mitigating the effect of 'sitting on the fence'. Although, generally speaking, English has a more rigorous internal logic than Hungarian, a missing piece of information becomes more glaringly obvious in Hungarian, e.g. calling someone a leader instead of giving his exact title, or saying 'earlier this month' or 'later this year'. And there is the difficulty of rendering opacity convincingly and of providing a plausible equivalent of waffle. All that is the stuff of compromise; Cervantes thought that a translation was inevitably the wrong side of a tapestry."

The problems of the translator (or translatoress, which must sound better in other languages than it does in English) impose strictures upon the writers of the English originals that the sections work from. We may expect our people to grope their way through the mist of English: to ask them to stumble blindly through a pea-souper is rather too much. Our news editors and script writers constantly need to remember to write in short simple sentences; avoid too many subordinate clauses; be precise (when the situation they are reporting is clear) rather than allusive; avoid metaphor – so easy to use, so difficult to translate; remember that assumptions acceptable for an English audience won't apply to a World Service one. Simple guidelines, but hard to stick to.

It is not difficult for the "entrenched positions" of Iraq and the USA to end up, literally, as "dug- outs" in translation. Describing a scientist as "an ardent motorcycle scrambler" may sound colourful in English: what is it going to mean to, say, the Vietnamese? And I treasure the *News About Britain* story on the Edinburgh Festival which, describing the particular year's attractions, blithely concluded with "...and of course the Searchlight Tattoo". Of course. Two words in English. Two lines in Slovene. And "a spectacular parade appearance of woodwind bands in Edinbugh Castle" is not a bad stab at encapsulating that particularly Scottish institution (even if the bagpipes weren't quite right).

It was only when glancing through Malcolm Bradbury's famous guidebook, *Why come to Slaka?* that I understood why I felt that I had known all about these problems for years. Where, you will ask, is Slaka? According to the guidebook it is "equidistantly placed between the Baltic and the Adriatic, the Danube and the Blub". The generous hand of nature has set it in a "warm and wooded declivity between the delightful Vronopian mountains... with the great Storkian plain to the East, and the rolled hills of the Pritprip to the west, fecundly watered by the great river Nyit which floods its proudish way through our verdant country."

As for the language, well if you know a bit of Finnish and Hittite, you will not be at a loss. In Bradbury's novel about Slaka, *Rates of Exchange*, a Slakan academic describes the language with all the conviction of any one of my 37 language service heads:

It is not so complicate. All you must know is the nouns end in 'i', or sometimes two or three, but with many exceptions. We have one spoken language and one book language. Really there are only three cases, but sometimes seven. Mostly it is inflected, but sometimes not. It is different from country to town, also from region to region because of our confused history. Vocabulary is a little bit Latin, a little bit German, a little bit Finn. So really it is quite simple. I think you will speak it very well, soon.

Translators then are not simply traitors. They are more complex than that. Jugglers, conjurers, mind readers, psychologists, games players, poets, social scientists. At the end they are cultural porters, offering the users of one language an imaginative equivalence of the meaning expressed in another. The question is not whether they get it wrong. The wonder is that so much of it is right.

First delivered to the Friends of Winchester College, on 6 March 1992.

CHAPTER 8

FOURTH ESTATE OR FIFTH COLUMN

THE MEDIA, THE GOVERNMENT AND THE STATE

N IGERIA is one of the most important target areas for the BBC World Service, giving us one of our largest and most loyal audiences. When last measured in 1989, we found that we had a regular audience in English of 11.7% or 7.2 million listeners. Research in the north of the country confirmed an audience for our Hausa broadcasts of 8.6 million. These figures represent our largest single national audience in English and our second largest audience in a non-English tongue. These are huge listening figures and we are very proud of them – well aware that they represent a responsibility as well as an obligation to us.

The well-known term "fourth estate" originated in a speech by Edmund Burke in the British Parliament. He noted the various estates of the realm: the Lords Spiritual, the Lords Temporal and the Commons – the powers that hold in their hands the ultimate destiny of British Governments. Then Burke added, pointing to the press gallery: "And yonder sits the Fourth Estate, more important than them all."

The phrase "fifth column" was first used by the Fascist General Mola, who said, during the Spanish Civil War in October 1936, that he was commanding five columns in the assault on Madrid; four converging on the city from various directions "and the fifth column within the city." It was Ernest Hemingway's use of the phrase in a play called *The Fifth Column* which established it permanently in the language as a reference to civilians subversively working in a clandestine fashion to undermine a regime or a state from within.

The idea of the media as the fourth estate, with its explicit connotation of a legitimate place in the constitution of the country, is a flattering one. The idea of the media as a fifth column is quite the reverse. Both cannot be true – or can they? I have yoked them together in an attempt to face the reality that while a public commitment to freedom of activity for the media is very general throughout the world – a commitment more honoured in the breach than in the observance – the acknowledgement that the media should have a quasi-legitimate constitutional position is weaker than it should be.

Allowance that if the media do have such a position, then they deserve to have it, is weaker still. Despite this recognition that the standing of the media – national or international – is not what it should be, I will argue first, that free media are essential to a healthy democracy – indeed are a condition of it; second, that governments and journalists have different objectives and that tension between them is inevitable; third, that the right to criticize and expose exercised by the press in a democracy carries a corresponding responsibility; fourth, that bad governments are far worse for their citizens than even the worst media.

Let me begin with history. For a century now, the power of the printed word has been clear for all to see. W.T. Stead, the Editor of the *Pall Mall Gazette*, wrote to his father in 1883: "Here am I, not yet thirty-five, and already the most influential man in England." Such status has not generally been granted to all journalists, or even to all organs of the press. It is said that a group of journalists were once introduced to a British Minister by his private secretary with the words: "Minister, the press and the Gentleman from the Times". In the 1960s, Harold Macmillan, the most quasi-aristocratic of Britain's recent leaders was asked what he thought of the press. He replied that they were all very well but they were "hardly the kind of people you would ask to the country for the weekend."

The new electronic broadcasting media initially adopted a posture of absurd deference to Ministers. In 1951, the British Prime Minister, Clement Attlee, was interviewed for television on his return from the United States. Attlee was a man of few words at the best of times:

INTERVIEWER *Good morning Mr. Attlee. We hope you've had
             a good journey.*
ATTLEE   *Yes, excellent.*

INTERVIEWER	Can you, now you're back, having cut short your lecture tour, tell us something of how you view the election prospects?
ATTLEE	Oh, we shall go in and have a good fight. A very good chance of winning, we shall go in confidently, we always do.
INTERVIEWER	And on what will Labour take its stand?
ATTLEE	Well, that we'll be announcing shortly.
INTERVIEWER	What are your immediate plans, Mr. Attlee?
ATTLEE	My immediate plan is to go down to a committee and decide on just that thing, as soon as I can get away from here.
INTERVIEWER	Anything else you'd care to say about the coming election?
ATTLEE	No.

We have advanced a good deal since then, whatever the difficulties we experience with questioning political leaders from time to time. The main objection to that interview – both to its questions and to its answers – is that it tells the audience, the democratic voters, absolutely nothing.

A still more celebrated instance of the stonewall interview occurred in 1962. The BBC Commonwealth Correspondent, Douglas Brown, met Nyasaland's Nationalist leader, Dr. Hastings Banda, on his arrival at London airport on 21st June 1962. This is how the interview – with the subsequent President of Malawi, preserved to this day in the BBC's archives – ran:

BROWN	Have you come here to ask the Secretary of State a firm date for Nyasaland independence?
BANDA	I won't tell you that.
BROWN	When do you hope to get independence?
BANDA	I won't tell you that.
BROWN	Dr. Banda, when you get independence are you as determined as ever to break away from the Central African Federation?
BANDA	Need you ask me that question at this stage?
BROWN	Well, this stage is as good as any other stage, why do you

> *ask why I shouldn't ask you this question at this stage?*
> BANDA   *Haven't I said enough for everybody to be convinced that I mean just that?*
> BROWN   *Dr. Banda, if you break with Central African Federation how will you make out economically. After all, your country isn't really a rich country ...?*
> BANDA   *Don't ask me that. Leave that to me.*
> BROWN   *But which way is your mind working?*
> BANDA   *Which way? I won't tell you that.*
> BROWN   *Where do you hope to get economic aid from?*
> BANDA   *I won't tell you that.*
> BROWN   *Are you going to tell me anything?*
> BANDA   *Nothing.*

By the 1970s, the role of the microphone interviewer as the deferential handmaiden of the interviewee had been dramatically altered – no longer a supplicant, more like an intruder. The former British Ambassador to Uruguay, Sir Geoffrey Jackson, one of the first victims of modern-day kidnapping at the hands of the Tupamaros in 1971, wrote of the change in the role of the reporters.

> *Before the war I had been drilled to an instant evasive reflex if the press ever hove into sight. Only the mighty ever confronted those coffin-like microphones of the early radio; television did not even exist to panic us. A decade later, we were to run with outstretched hand to meet the press. On tour from overseas headquarters we were not to shrink from the intrusive hand-mike, or to wince at the inevitable question 'What does it feel like ...'*

The idea that the media are troublesome to diplomats and politicians is long-standing. It is shared by governments of all shades, both democratic and totalitarian. The Emperor Napoleon once said that "Four newspapers are more to be feared than a thousand bayonets". There is a Russian joke which has Napoleon say to Stalin that if he had had a newspaper like *Pravda*, nobody would ever have known of his defeat at Waterloo in 1815. Clearly the French – great believers in the importance of central authority – continue to have a cautious view of what to do with the media.

In the early 1960s, President de Gaulle asked President Jack Kennedy: "How can you control your country if you do not control television?" Many American Presidents since must have asked themselves that very question.

What is implicit in those questions is the view on the part of government that the media are at best a nuisance, at worst dangerous and that they should be subject to state regulation, control or manipulation; but it is – for the most part – only implicit. Others present a view of the imperative need to regulate the media in a more direct way. That theoretician and practitioner of the control of state power, Lenin, declared his highly qualified view of press freedom in 1920: "Publishing enterprises must not be permitted to abuse their autonomy by pursuing a policy that is not entirely party policy". Information, communication and comment were, according to Lenin, too important to be left to the merely bourgeois so-called freedoms of the press and, by natural extension, the electronic media. But you do not have to be an autocratic ideologue, such as Lenin, to raise questions about the role of the media. That extraordinary Russian religious nationalist and anti-communist dissident, Alexander Solzhenitsyn, mused:

> The press has become the greatest power within western countries; more powerful than the legislature, the executive and the judiciary. One would like to ask: by what law has it been elected and to whom is it responsible?

Let me take three cases where government and an element of the media have come into conflict and examine what both sides said at the time. In 1852 The Times, then most truly deserving its name of The Thunderer, was engaged in a robust disagreement with that most buccaneering of British Foreign Secretaries and the founder of gunboat diplomacy, Lord Palmerston. Defending his Minister, the Prime Minister, Lord Derby, gave The Times a sharp pull on the reins. He did not like the sight of newspapers telling his Foreign Secretary how to run foreign policy. According to Lord Derby:

> As in these days the English Press aspires to share the influences of statesmen, so also must it share in the responsibilities of statesmen.

The challenge is clear enough; if you want to meddle in these affairs, then you must become part of the process which shares them. The then editor of *The Times*, Delane, instructed Robert Lowe to reply at length and in detail. Lowe conceded that if the first part of Lord Derby's proposition were true – that the press wanted to have the same influence as ministers – then the second – that it should accept the same responsibilities as ministers – would certainly follow. But Lowe challenged Derby's proposition about the relationship between what he called the two powers, government and press:

> *The purposes and duties of the two powers are constantly separate, generally independent, sometimes diametrically opposite. The dignity and the freedom of the Press are trammelled from the moment it accepts an ancillary position. To perform its duties with entire independence, and consequently with the utmost public advantage, the Press can enter into no close or binding alliances with the statesmen of the day, nor can it surrender its permanent interests to the convenience of the ephemeral power of any Government.*

The following day, *The Times* returned to the theme as it certainly deserved. In a leader, it declared that the press must roam freely over topics that men of action dare not touch. (I would add that there is nothing wrong about this, nothing disreputable about a plain difference of function.) *The Times* went on:

> *Governments must treat other governments with external respect, however bad their origin or foul their deeds; but happily the Press is under no such trammels, and, while diplomatists are exchanging courtesies, can unmask the mean heart that beats beneath a star, or point out the bloodstains on the hand which grasps a sceptre. The duty of the journalist is the same as that of the historian – to seek out truth, above all things, and to present to his readers not such things as statecraft would wish them to know but the truth as near as he can attain it … To require, then, the journalist and the statesman to conform to the same rules is to mix up things essentially different, and is as unsound in theory as unheard of in practice.*

115

I believe *The Times* was right then and its conclusions are still valid today. If the responsibilities of the media are no different from the responsibilities of the government then there is no need for the media at all, but merely the activities of a Ministry of Information.

But to purvey information to the public on such a basis is to perpetrate a fraud on the citizens – they are not receiving independent reporting but a partial and self-serving view of events – and ultimately leads to a situation where the government believes its own propaganda untrammelled by any counter-balancing point of view. That is no sort of formula for good government and more and more countries are coming to realise it.

One of the most celebrated clashes between the media and the government in recent times occurred over the Vietnam War in the United States. The Nixon administration, trying to extricate the United States from a disastrous war which was losing any support it had had among the American people, decided it must attack the instrument that was helping the steady loss of credibility of Administration policy: the tv network news shows. The person chosen for this selective moral strike on the media was Vice-President Spiro Agnew, (who later pleaded guilty to income tax evasion, was fined $10,000 and put on probation for three years).

In 1969 he launched into a general attack on what he called the television establishment: "A small group of men, numbering per-haps no more than a dozen 'anchormen', commentators, and executive producers," who "live and work in the geographical and intellectual confines of Washington, D.C., or New York City", and whose capacity for choosing what forty or fifty million people learned each day through television concerning national and international affairs represented "a concentration of power over American public opinion unknown in history."

Agnew overlooked the fact that the three network news shows were in deadly competition with one another, that their search for competitively different journalistic presentation was hardly conducive to sharing the same line, and that the public could – as they have often done – vote with their switches. Agnew personalised his attack on one correspondent in particular, Daniel Schorr of CBS News. He and others, claimed the Vice-President,

116

made up "a tiny, enclosed fraternity of privileged men elected by no-one and enjoying a monopoly sanctioned and licensed by government."

It is curious that Alexander Solzhenitsyn and Spiro Agnew – surely with nothing else in common – share one query: "Who elects the media?" Schorr was very direct in his reply to the Agnew attacks. The argument was not only a matter of principle; it was undoubtedly a matter of power:

> *I think we've come to the point where big concentrations of power can be controlled only by other big concentrations of power. Just as it would take the federal government to control the oil industry, which even its power hasn't succeeded in doing yet, so it takes big news organisations to stand up to big government, with a lot of power.*

But the issue of the distribution of power itself conceals a major question of principle. In a democracy, power is diffused; in the United States even formally separated. The power of the media is one way of creating a necessary alternative counter to what would otherwise be an over-concentration of power. In the course of the controversy over the tv networks' coverage of the Vietnam War, Frank Stanton – President of CBS –made a speech in Utah in July 1970 warning that the delicate mechanism governing the interaction between government and a reasonably well–informed public might be thrown out of balance:

> *If the words and views of the President become a monolithic force, if they constitute not just the powerful voice in the land but the only one speaking for a nationwide point of view.*

Stanton was stating a basic principle. All leaders hope that they speak for the people, that they articulate the hopes, dreams, wishes of a nation. If they are great leaders, that is exactly what they must try to do, and sometimes manage to do. But they cannot take the achievement for granted. They must earn it. And they cannot snatch it by suppressing all those inconvenient voices which call into question their claims to be the sole, unchallenged national voice. The media are inconvenient – they get in the way. But they do so not just because, congenitally, they are members of the awkward squad but because national leaders need to have their claims to unquestioning legitimacy and authority – to be the sole arbiters of their nation's destiny – subjected to constant, critical test.

Surely this assertion hardly needs testing itself. Modern history is littered with instances of leaders who claimed to speak for their people and then killed those who challenged that right. The magnitude of their failure is matched only by the scale of their presumption, the grandiosity of their projects and the size of the tragedy they visited on their people.

> *My name is Ozymandias, King of Kings*
> *Look on my Works, ye Mighty, and Despair!*

Who has killed more people throughout the Twentieth Century? The most mendacious ruler, unchallenged by the media? Or the most exploitative and venal media baron, unregulated by a government? In such a contest, the only one that matters, there is no contest. But the argument will not rest there. What responsibility does the media have to the state? Some journalists think the press has no responsibility whatsoever to the authorities that are in place. The press is answerable, says this school of thought, only to its readers, or audience.

Lord Annan, the distinguished British academic who was the chairman of the official enquiry into broadcasting in the United Kingdom in March 1977, maintains that the state must be brought into the picture. "It is the legal expression of the nation; repository of sovereignty; sole source of legal cohesion; source of authority of the armed forces; agent of law." For Annan the state is:

> *quite different from the Government... The State is our nation: Monarchy, Parliament, Judiciary, Ministers. It is the entity which demands our loyalty, which the Government has no right to demand, except of course from the members of a political party who belong to it. Each of us owes duties to the State because it is the State which defines and sustains our rights through the laws of the*

country. And it demands our loyalty because, through the armed forces and the police, it alone can defend us from invasion or anarchy.

I have no disagreement with that. Annan then attempts to connect that principle with a definition of how the media should share their action in response to it:

Broadcasters owe a duty to the State. Broadcasters should remember that they owe a duty to the reputations of politicians ... statements which discredit not merely the politician but the whole concept of government, without which a society cannot exist, destroy public confidence in the nation in a peculiarly poisonous way.

I recognise the argument and admit most of it. But it is not conclusive in the way that Lord Annan appeared to think it was. What should the broadcaster do if the very foundation of the state is unjust? In posing the question, I do not arrogate to the broadcaster/journalist the duty to question constantly the justice of the foundations of the state. But, as Lord Annan put it, there is something very British, very settled, very smug about the dichotomy between the government – whose actions should be monitored – and the state – whose basis guarantees us, the British, our very freedoms. Of course, a state which gives citizens its basic freedoms and protection, including the freedom of expression both public and private, deserves and requires a special respect. What of one which does none of these things?

Even before the democracy movement in Eastern Europe, the Soviet Union and now in Africa, it was clear that there were many states which made claims to give their citizens fundamental rights, but who did nothing of the kind in practice. What kind of duty do the media owe to a state which not only does not guarantee basic rights but actually violates them? Must the broadcaster bend the knee to an entity merely because it calls itself a state and thereby apparently puts itself on to a higher plane of being in the removed world of political theory?

According to this view, the Soviet Union, the state of Stalin's purges, of Brezhnevite stagnation, of massive historic oppression and injustice, should not have been challenged because it was the state. The media have no choice but to ask questions about the government of the day or the state of the moment, not because they are special, not because they are better, not because they are arrogant, not because they are self-appointed, but because if they do not do it, nobody else will. Nobody else, that is to say, until the people themselves, their spirits freed by the prior releasing of their media, take matters into their own hands as they did in the velvet revolutions of eastern Europe in 1989.

So what is the responsibility of the journalist? It is to report evenly, accurately, to tell the truth. Democracy is a hollow word unless those who exercise their right to vote have the facts on which to base their choice at the ballot-box. The great British nineteenth-century writer on the Constitution, Walter Bagehot, warned:

Knowledge will forever govern ignorance. And a people who mean to be their own governors must arm themselves with the proper power that knowledge gives. A popular government without a popular information or the means of acquiring it, is but a prologue to a farce or tragedy, or perhaps both.

During a recent trip to Czechoslovakia I heard the Director of Czechoslovak Radio, Frantisek Pavlicek, apologize to his people for allowing lies to be told to them over the past thirty years: "I am sorry. I ask you to accept this apology. I ask you to forgive us for all the lies, insults and odium". The influential American columnist Walter Lippmann wrote:

The theory of a free press is that the truth will emerge from free reporting and discussion – not that it will be presented perfectly and instantly in any one account.

As Lippmann realised, the path to truth is an arduous one and many stumble on the way. It needs single-minded devotion on the part of the prospector. He or she cannot serve another cause at the same time, such as being a propagandist for the state, a party or a cause. But to make a single mistake or even several, does not undermine the argument for independent journalism. It is a logical fallacy to argue as some politicians do that the commission of a single editorial error destroys all credibility. It merely shows that the participant is human, not that what they are trying to do is invalid. Repeated errors of a pre-ordained and deliberate kind are very different. "To err is human, to forgive divine." But, as George Bernard Shaw wrote: "To err is human, to persevere diabolical." Lippmann recognised that it is the process of honest inquiry that matters. The process itself, if honestly undertaken and honestly maintained, will produce a decent result, despite the errors, the moments off balance. It will survive the nit-picking. For the process is far greater than the specific challenge which calls it into question.

One of my BBC colleagues, Colin Morris, a great Methodist preacher, has graphically sketched the conditions under which the broadcaster works:

> In the Book of Genesis, it is God who brings order out of chaos; in the modern world, television journalists have to make a stab at doing it. They subdue into harmony a mountain of telex print-outs, miles of video tape and a pandemonium of ringing telephones. They organise into a coherent picture a riot of impressions, a chaos of events, a bedlam of attitudes and opinions that would otherwise send us scurrying to the hills in a panic. And they have to construct this world view at lightning speed, in a welter of instant judgements. Not for them the luxury afforded to philosophers of earlier ages who could reflect at leisure on the fitness of things. Aristotle had no six o'clock deadline to meet.

Morris goes on to suggest that the work of the journalist is, in a fundamental sense, religious: "Is not the word 'religion' derived from a Latin root, 'religare', 'to tie together' or 'to bind'? And is not this what the journalist does as he or she knits together verbal and visual symbols into some semblance of reality?"

My former distinguished colleague was undoubtedly overstating the case. Even in our most optimistic moments, broadcasters would not in the main argue that our function is quasi-religious. But we would argue that the activity of the media gives a cohesion to society, a cohesion based on freely delivered information, easily received and consent to government openly granted, leading to a more decent society.

I am well aware that these claims do not resonate with recent African theory, experience or some current inclination. Governments feel weak rather than strong, threatened by tribal rivalries, economic failure, ideological disputes, religious tensions. In such an atmosphere, the response has been to demand of the journalist / broadcaster in Africa that they should indeed live up to the definition offered by Colin Morris – that they should bind the nation together and that criticism, dissent, investigation, all the customary activities of the media should take second place to the primary need of national unity.

As Paul Ansah of the University of Ghana has written in *Index on Censorship* in October 1981:

> *African governments find it necessary to control broadcasting operations in order to promote national unity, socio-economic development and stability. It is felt that if control is not exercised, there is the danger of the system falling into the hands of a group of wealthy people who could use it to promote commercial, sectional or political interests that may be at variance with national objectives.*

President Kaunda, who has just set an admirable example of the democratic process at work, said in 1968:

> *The international press qualifies as one of the many invisible governments. The press is capable of making or destroying governments given appropriate conditions, it can cause war or create conditions for peace. It can promote development or create difficulties in the way of development.*

That is an inflated idea of the power of the Western media. It confuses cause and consequence, but it shows the concern and suspicion with which many African leaders view it.

That pioneer of independent rule, Kwame Nkrumah, was preoccupied with the role of the media in his new state. Nkrumah maintained that the press must be under party and government control. His was a Leninist view of the function of the journalist. In the capitalist media, according to Nkrumah, the writer:

> ....finds himself rejecting or destroying facts that do not coincide with the outlook and interest of his employer or the medium's advertisers ... trivialities are blown up, the vulgar emphasised, ethics forgotten, the important trimmed to the class outlook...the true African journalist very often works for the cause of the political party to which he himself belongs and in whose purpose he believes. He works to serve a society moving in the direction of his aspirations.

There are many in Africa who argue that the press has a special role in addition to the tasks of informing and entertaining. For these people, writes Paul Ansah:

> the press in a developing country is expected to help forge a sense of national unity, identity and integration and to mobilise the people for development. Many leaders in developing countries also consider that it is their responsibility to provide information to citizens as a social service in the same way as they provide other services such as educational, health and recreational facilties.

I recognise the fears; I do not accept the remedies. For a start, there cannot be two different codes of journalistic ethics: a higher set of editorial standards for the developed world and a looser discipline for the developing nations seems to me to be ultimately unacceptable. It is as dangerous to accept such a differentiation as it would be to set different standards for surgeons or aircraft maintenance. It is patronising on the part of the West, defeatist on the side of the Third World. It is a disservice to those who look to the media for a true picture of events, and it is harmful to the democratic process. It handicaps young talent and blights the lives of those who try to report honestly and fully.

A free press is the mark of a confident nation; an accurate press is the sign of a mature people; a press which can criticize governments temperately and governments which react rationally to such criticism, are evidence of a civilised state. Arrest warrants for editors who point to the gap between words and deeds expose frightened rulers. The response to media which trivialise and sensationalise is best left to their audience.

Finally, in defence of my argument, let me quote once more from that robust apologia for the Fourth Estate written by Robert Lowe in *The Times* 140 years ago:

> *The first duty of the Press is to obtain the earliest and most correct intelligence of the events of the time, and instantly, by disclosing them, to make them the common property of the nation. The statesman collects his information secretly and by secret means; he keeps back even the current intelligence of the day with ludicrous precautions, until diplomacy is beaten in the race with publicity.*

I find it enormously heartening that a defence of freedom of information made almost 150 years ago still resounds with such strength and relevance today. It suggests to me that the principles which I have tried to articulate are well rooted in soil so eloquently dug over by Robert Lowe and many others after him.

> *For us, with whom publicity and truth are the air and light of existence, there can be no greater disgrace than to recoil from the frank and accurate disclosure of facts as they are. We are bound to tell the truth as we find it, without fear of consequences – to lend no convenient shelter to acts of injustice and oppression, but to consign them at once to the judgment of the world.*

To those still in doubt, I offer only this sad observation and challenge. Where were the free media when Pol Pot slaughtered millions in Cambodia? Where were the free media when Idi Amin killed millions in Uganda? Where were the free media when Hitler sent millions of Jews to the concentration camps? Where were the free media when Stalin carried out his purges and created his gulags? The answer is simple – they were silenced. This is no mere rhetorical flourish. Those who argue – on the most reasonable grounds – for a docile, silent media, must ask whether the silence this will lead to is not the silence of the grave.

The media are the Fourth Estate of government, in a plural, democratic society. In a tyranny, they may well be a Fifth Column – which sets out to destroy the very basis of an unjust, oppresive state. Fourth Estate or Fifth Column – it is not an antithesis, it is a choice. The media can be both at the same time.

And quite right too.

First delivered at the Nigerian Institute of International Affairs, Lagos, on November 12th, 1991.

CHAPTER 9
FOURTH ESTATE OR FIRST VICTIMS
NIGERIA DIARY

SUNDAY NOVEMBER 10. The experience of Nigeria starts at Gatwick. Allocation of seats is only finalised at the last minute, because there are so many variables – of the human kind. BA regard it as a nightmare flight to despatch. Today's human variables include a sad group of five deportees who naturally take first priority on returning flights. In the rough modern world of air travel, they are never the ones who will be "bumped". They sit sad, forlorn, dejected, as an Immigration official says briskly, but not heavily: "Come on now, you all know what the situation is, so let's get on board". Accompanied by him and just two BA women ground staff, almost like VIP treatment, they walk on to the plane passively. At least they are not going back to persecution or arrest.

Six hours later at Lagos, the lights are out in one part of the airport, so we stumble along the aircraft pier lit by occasional torches. In the baggage hall, one of the baggage conveyors is stripped down to its steel skeleton, all the rubber moving pads removed. Jim Whittell – my host from the British Council – explains that this is a response to the President's call to the nation to repair and maintain.

Monday November 11. First official meeting is with the Minister of Information, Chief Alex Akinyele. I should have known better what to expect – not a quiet, private dialogue about the media and government information: an ambush, just like similiar occasions in Kenya – with the late, lamented Foreign Minister, Robert Ouko – or in Uganda, with the Information Minister. As Jim and I enter the conference room, I see a tv camera, at least half a dozen journalists, and in no time three microphones lie on the table in front of us.

After a few minutes, Akinyele sweeps in and is immediately on camera. He is large, dressed in blue silk agbada and shawl, beautifully embroidered, perfectly ironed with razor sharp creases. In no time, he is delivering an official potted history of Nigeria. "There has not been a single coup in modern times that the people have not welcomed". I forbear to ask about last year's failed coup against Babangida for which many died. He talks of the free press, of their criticism and openness. I ask if they are critical of him? "Of course, they caricature me, they cartoon me, they attack me". Does he keep the cartoons? "Of course," he shrieks to hoots of laughter from the journalists. "Bring the files" he tells his staff, who then scurry in over the next ten minutes with further cases of anti- Alex drawings. They are sharp, no question.

What cannot the media cover, I ask. "They can report anything, so long as they do not damage national security, national unity and national integrity". Well, we are already on tricky ground where individual definitions can vary a great deal. As time runs on, Alex recalls the cameras are on and prepares for his homily at the BBC. As these things go, it is a comparatively mild version of the homily I have already heard in Kenya and Uganda. After praise for the BBC in general, he asks for "support" for Nigeria's development in our journalism. I explain that while we aim to provide coverage, knowledge of the area and therefore sympathy for its condition, we cannot act as advocates for its development if that means not reporting what is going on inside the country. Alex latches onto the word "sympathy" and confers on it a weight of overt support that I did not intend. I clarify what I see as our role – which is far removed from a commitment of our support for their development policies. Who knows how many of my reservations will appear in the final edited tv/radio versions...

(The following evening a former politician at Christopher Macrae's dinner at the British High Commission takes me aside. "My daughter heard Akinyele's remarks to you about the BBC on the radio". "Did they include my answer?" I asked, knowing the reply. "No" he said. "But my daughter asked me to tell you that she and many people she knows disagree with what Akinyele said to you."

Clearly Alex is something of an issue in Nigeria. At the same Macrae dinner I sit next to two leading Nigerian journalists. Towards the end of the dinner one of them asks: "Confidentially, what do you think of our Information Minister?" I look around, think and say: "Confidentially, I think you deserve better". They nod and agree. "If you have to have an Information Minister, then it should be done well and in such a way that he brings respect to the nation and also to the press. As it is he does the Nigerian press no good". This is music to their ears, though a sad kind of music. "Apart from anything else," I say, "I was invited to a private meeting with Alex. I did not expect to be plunged into a one way tv news hijack, which is what happened". I did not say that this treatment was now par for the course in Africa in my experience. In one sense I do not mind it; it shows a readiness on the part of the BBC to take it as well as to hand it out. But at some stage African governments are going to have to learn that this is no way to treat the media. What it reflects is a contempt for the media and a belief, perhaps unadmitted, that in relations with the media anything is permissible.)

However, Chief Alex has enjoyed himself so much that we are late reaching Chief Tom Ikimi, Chairman of the National Republican Convention, the "right" leaning of the two officially authorised parties in the transition to democracy. Ikimi – another big man in a beautiful white agbada and shawl greets us in a smallish house on Victoria Island crammed with objects. The first sight as I enter the living room is of four stuffed leopards lying on the ground as welcoming party. Behind them two of the largest mounted elephant tusks conceivable, massive crescents of yellow ivory. Behind a dividing screen, four more tusks, elaborately carved. Colourful Nigerian paintings crowd the walls, three terracotta figures of a jazz band stand on the tv, a row of Nigerian terracotta heads line the wall, a bookcase filled with videos.

Ikimi appears a nice man, intelligent, calm, but not necessarily a razor intellect, still less an overpowering political talent. But he has left the sheltered life of architecture for the rough and occasionally fatal life of Nigerian politics, and since he does not need the money – with a house in Hampstead Garden Suburb and children educated in an English girls' public school – he should get credit for some public idealism. Ikimi claims to be sure of the NRC's victory next year but is well aware of the scale of the difficulties in the democratic road ahead. He describes the differences between the two artificial parties, ideologically defined, which the military have decreed shall form the basis of the new democratic politics. "The SDP talk about equality, a just society, distribution, sharing of oil revenues and so on. We talk of using the oil to provide growth, to develop, to give opportunities."

A 90 minute drive to Otta to the west of Lagos to see General Obasanjo. Like Cincinnatus, he has retired to his farm on leaving office. He cuts a large and splendid figure on international tv screens, always carefully appearing in splendid Nigerian robes. He is part of the elder statesmen's travelling road show, but with his hat in the ring for the UN Secretary General his ambitions are far from dead.

On his farm, he is relaxed, wearing a bright purple pyjama suit and hat, kicking off his leather slippers, lolling back comfortably in an arm chair. He talks slowly, listing his ideas in numbered groups of four, sometimes pausing so long that it is not clear if he is finished or not. I get the impression that he is regarded as a "good soldier" – he took power but gave it up quickly and honourably. He talks for democracy and the rule of law in Africa. (I have just offended a young Nigerian politician sitting next to me on the flight to Kano. He was so obviously looking at what I was writing that I had to angle the screen away from him somewhat too obviously. He gave a little moan of disappointment or disapproval and leaned in the other direction.)

Obasanjo is frank about the lessons of running the farm. He went to it because he wanted to offer another example to young Nigerians beyond going into business or commerce. For six years it went well. Then he found that interest rates on his loans shot up to 30%, while the recession reduced the number of poor Nigerians who could buy a chicken. He has capacity for 200,000 chicks, and running a farm with that capacity at a level of 50,000 chicks was ruinous. Finally he found that banks could not be relied on to understand farming; if you have just bought 20,000 live chicks, they cannot be stored away for future use until the bank decides if the risk is good. However he is still there. He talks regularly to local secondary schools about democracy and the rule of law. A local headmaster is in the outer waiting room, and thanks him for coming to talk. "Was it too high for them?" ask Obasanjo. "Maybe a little" replies the headmaster, "but that is good, it will make them think".

Over a simple lunch of farm chicken – a cut above UK battery chicken – he says he has no wish to go back to government and says why he is anxious about the transition to democracy. It is not clear what the military's real intentions are, or if the return to democracy will work smoothly in practice. He is very worried about the inclinations of the military – too many of them want to get into the army in order to get into government. It is widespread gossip that young officers discuss among themselves what Governorships each will have. There is anxiety about the sheer money orientation of the civilians now coming into politics, some of them thought to be tainted with drugs money.

Is there anything positive? Long pause. He sucks a chicken bone and decides that the people's wish to get the military out is the most important factor in the scene. But I suppose that the anti-military feeling of the present must be set against memories of the failings of the politicians from the past.

On the way back from Otta we stop in Ikeja for a discussion session with senior journalists on the *Nigerian Daily Times*. About a dozen of the NDT's senior editors join me and the Editor in Chief, Yemi Ogibunye, for an exchange of views. I get the full range of queries: are we in the pocket of the FCO? Doesn't Mrs Thatcher's pressure on the BBC show it is not independent? Why does the

BBC only recruit from Oxbridge and not from the working class universities? Does not the BBC broadcast only a middle class agenda ignoring working people? (Nice to find classical Marxism alive and kicking.) Why does the BBC only cover negative African stories? Why cannot the BBC sympathise with and be positive about Nigerian development? Does the vetting of BBC staff not prove that we are in the pockets of the secret services? It was a good dry run for further questions on the same lines throughout.

Tuesday November 12. A start with Chief Humphrey Nwosu, Chairman of the National Election Commission or NEC. Nwosu is large, expansive and virtually impossible to stop. He lives in a world of system and scheme. He described a vast pyramid of voting that the NEC was setting up. At over 220,000 voting stations – each one with no more than 500 people due to vote there – officials, policemen, party officials would count and ratify the vote "declaring it with a loud voice" before passing it on the the next level where more officials would count, sign, ratify and authenticate the vote – and "declare it with a loud voice". It was all like "Athenian democracy". By the end he admitted that it would need a million people just to administer the vote alone, prompting the cynical thought that more might be involved in administering the elections than in voting in them. Nwosu is sensitive at suggestions that the so-called "open ballot" – or queueing behind the list of your chosen candidate – comes from Kenya, where it was undoubtedly used to intimidate voters. This is a Nigerian way he insisted. The people were so disgusted at the way the parties had abused the secret ballot that they welcomed the open ballot – no doubt as they welcomed the military coups themselves.

Nwosu leaves us with a sense of unreality. He is an Ibo. At the Nigerian Television Authority, where the leadership is Hausa, his name draws a striking response. Nwosu has talked a lot about "social mobilisation" in the context of the electoral process. So I asked the NTA editors and Directors how much they were doing about social mobilisation? Much rolling of heads and heaving of bodies. "We are projecting Nwosu a lot. He is the most over-exposed man in Nigeria. When the people see him they switch off".

I go off to do a sixty-minute interview on the NTA Dialogue spot, being cross examined by their Head of Current Affairs Programmes and three journalists. The studio air conditioning has broken down and the small studio is insufferably hot. But the whole experience is remarkably enjoyable. They interview well, very forthrightly, and to a fairly predictable line, but they have done their homework and they are direct without being rude. One of the men coins a marvellous paranoid phrase about the international media – "international media terrorism". I think this is a bit rich and say so. The whole thing is a fair corrective to the Akinyele experience but all it shows is that journalists are better trained professionally than the Ministers. That is the problem. I emerge drenched and exhausted.

Back home to rest before the lecture. I crash out for an hour and only just have time to revise the lecture and introduce a number of cuts for time. The Nigerian Institute of International Affairs is a purpose built research centre. George Obiozor, a large ebullient noisy Ibo, is the Director. I am not quite sure how the lecture will go down though suppose most will at least be well disposed to the idea of a free press.

The hall is packed – 400 seating and more standing. I have subbed hard to get the length right. What about the tone? They laugh at the first joke. They pick up the first not too heavy irony. I know they are an alert sharp audience. It goes well. Very intelligent questions afterwards and we break up at 6.15 after 30 minutes of questions. A lively crowd afterwards outside the hall. Many are young, eager. One says: "Fourth estate or fifth column, yes. But in the Third World the media are something else – they are the first victims of government". What a marvellous phrase, I say. "Please remember where you heard it first", he said.

After that I really am exhausted but after a quick bath, off to the Macrae's for dinner. The turnout is even more blue-chip than the previous evening dinner at the Whittell's with the Finance Minister, the Minister of Justice, presidential hopefuls, and editors arriving in glittering traditional costume. Having met some in western suits, I did not always recognize them in traditional agboda, especially with their hats on. I arrive early to talk to a former governor Agbo Ike who could not stay for the dinner. Like most of the disqualified politicians he is articulate, intelligent and serious minded. He is scathing about the so-called "open ballot". It removes the decency of the secret ballot from the people. It is easy to manipulate. Many will not put up with standing in queues for the time needed. Already examples of rigging have been developed and put into practice. He sees it as an alien import of highly dubious origin.

He is forgiving about his imprisonment – for over two years. Despite enquiries, no one ever convicted him, as Governor, of bribery. They did say that in his role as Governor he should have known that his subordinates were corrupt. That is certainly taking the doctrine of Ministerial responsibility in its classic sense to a high degree. He has just written a book about his time in jail, during which he kept a secret radio and listened regularly and devotedly to the World Service.

Over dinner I commit a spectacular gaffe with my attractive Nigerian woman neighbour. "What is your job?" I ask, thinking that that is far better than asking "What does your husband do?" She says: "Why do you ask me that question?". "It seems preferable to any of the alternatives. What should I have said?" "Nothing, really." "Oh well, let's stick with the first one. What is your job?" "I sell pesticides in the market. They even come from Togo to buy pesticides from me". Later I ask someone to decode the conversation. "Well, to start with you should have asked her where she comes from. That's essential in Nigeria. Then, when she talks of the market, she is not a stall trader. She is probably a big business trader". There is a near disaster of protocol when some of the guests say they want to watch my interview on NTA at 10pm, some even say they would like to get home to see it. Fortunately Metta Macrae is very relaxed and unfazed and the promise of cassettes for everyone keeps them at the table until its proper end. A warm speech of welcome from Chris Macrae. I reply by saying that two hours of public speaking in one day has surely tried the patience of all. Thank you is enough – and I mean it.

Wednesday 13 November. To Kano. Footnotes to the Nigerian Institute lecture. A week ago a World Bank Vice President, Lawrence Summers, delivered a very blunt, outspoken speech to the NIA. He coined the word "kleptocracy" to describe all too many African governments, without mentioning Nigeria by name. Worse still – he called them the thirteenth poorest nation in the world. Two consequences: no one took up the damaging charge of kleptocracy, and everyone took offence at and concentrated on the "thirteenth poorest nation" figure.

The speech got virtually no coverage at all. This can be a sensitive audience. After my speech, laden with books and a commemorative plaque, I start walking off the platform. One of my hosts insists that I must hand over the pile to a servant. He points to a servant-looking Nigerian and tells him to carry my swag. Net result is that the man vanishes and neither my swag nor my corrected and amended speech are seen for several days. So much for being treated like a "Big Man".

Air travel in Nigeria is a very local matter. To get me to Kano, Jim has despatched Thomson the British Council fixer to the airport to fix. Rajiv, the new office manager, accompanies me and Ganyu the driver. Then on second thoughts Rajiv is new and does not know his way around the airport. So Larry, another office manager, is sent too. I think this must be over-egging the pudding, but then I do not know Nigeria.

The traffic is bad. Left to himself, Ganyu would take the main road and sweat it out. Larry urges another route. This too is choc-a-bloc. We take short cuts through back streets to avoid bottle necks and reach the airport at 10 am, the re-scheduled time of departure for the Okada Air flight. Or was it 10.45 on the original schedule but nobody told us? Since deregulation, various private airlines have grown up because of the sheer awfulness of Nigerian Airways. These operate out of a small one-storey building crammed with market and news stalls, but none of the trappings of an air terminal such as ticket desks, baggage checking facilities and still less boarding cards.

Thomson, the Council's permanent fixer, has done all of that – God knows where – thrusts me into a damp executive lounge and when the tannoy announces the Kano flight five minutes later, Thomson re-appears, grabs my case and we set off at a run. The domestic air tarmac is like a bus station. Ten planes – mainly antique BAC 1-11s – are parked there and the tarmac is criss-crossed with passengers running to find their plane without any signs or directions to help them. Okada Air; Kabo Air; ADC; Concord Air – naturally they fly Fokker Friendships. Somehow they end up at the right plane – how many do not? – and queue up in front of a destination sign which is only visible once you have found the correct plane. This is the age of free seating, i.e. a mad scramble.

Thomson however is at the head of the queue. We wait. An official at the foot of the steps beckons me to come over. "You are from the BBC?" "Yes." "Can you please tell me why I cannot get any copies of *London Calling*? I used to get it for years. Now it has stopped". I explain that it is probably due to the fact that we have gone over to a subscription system but promise to look into it. "Thank you. I am a regular listener to the BBC. I am black, but also British".

We wait thirty minutes while the visibility clears at Kano due to the hamatan – the sandy, mist bearing wind that comes in from the Sahara at this time of the year and restricts flying. Over Kano the visibility is certainly very hazy. The pilot seems to circle more than he should and finally makes a long low approach which at times gives the impression that he is peering through the sand haze to find the airport. But at last the wheels go down and we are down an hour late. The air is dry, and you can smell the sand off the Sahara.

Fenella Brooks from Lagos who has organised my tour, and the British Council Kano rep, David Feiller, meet me and whisk me straight off to the offices of the local paper, the *Triumph* – both the Daily and the Sunday variety. The Editor gathers his senior colleagues and we are off for another session on journalism, independence and of course the BBC. They reflect feelings about Gulf coverage more than journalists in Lagos but of course it was our Hausa service whose listeners voted Saddam Hussein Man of the Year last year, to the intense irritation of the desk officers at the FCO. But after all the questioning, the doubts, the suspicion, they all say in one form or another, "we all listen to the BBC; rely on the BBC; monitor the BBC; get our news from the BBC."

It is like a love-hate, quasi-parental relationship where the dominant parent is both loved and respected. I have always said that our listeners are critical and cannot be fooled. Everyone I have spoken to in this heartland of our audience bears this out. It is very encouraging – both the loyalty and the questioning. But there is one misunderstanding that keeps cropping up. Because Mrs Thatcher criticised the BBC, they assume that we were not free to broadcast as we thought right. I reply that politicians will always query the media, more or less robustly. That does not mean that the press is restricted. What they must do is to watch how the press respond to the criticism, and I maintain, as I believe, that we have not been intimidated. It is an intelligent, rewarding discussion. The following day the papers report it in fair detail with absolute accuracy.

The manager of Kano Radio is another kettle of fish. I endure – it is past two o'clock now – the usual complaints which come out as whingeing. RFI (Radio France International) and VOA (Voice of America) give them music tapes, so why don't we? DW (Deutsche Welle) give them training so why don't we? When he talks of our coverage of Africa and South Africa as negative, I lose my patience. BBC reporters reported the ANC struggle with apartheid in full and at the risk of life and limb. They were faced with expulsion, we were faced with closure, as we told Africa what was happening in the main issue of the continent. While I was about it, on the question of fair treatment of Africa, I was getting tired of being misused by African Ministers of Information. I described my treatment by Chief Alex and said I thought the likes of him had a great deal to learn.

The Editor said that they were going to be fair by giving me a 20 minute interview. A youngish man does a very good and searching job. He never looks me in the eyes once. I wonder if he is getting signals from the cubicle but Fenella says it is a matter of respect. It would be wrong of him to look a "big man" like me directly in the eyes.

There are few signs in Kano of the recent riots and sectarian killings. One large poster on the way from the airport still proclaims the mission of the Christian fundamentalist, Reinhard Bonnke. David Feiller sums up the events like this: no one objected to the visit of Bonnke in itself. When pamphlets and leaflets were printed in Hausa, making it clear that he was intent on conversion, the Muslims asked for it to be stopped. It was not. Very young Muslims, possibly egged on by local villains from the market, then started the attack on the Christians. They were armed to a degree, reasonably well organised, and set up barricades. Nevertheless a lot were killed on both sides, probably half and half. How many? The government still says six. Public estimates rise to, say, thirty. David told of one local doctor who reliably assessed it at 1,000. But he had not been able to see the whole picture. He now inclined to the view that the deaths might have been as high as 3,000. No one believes the government figure. Only the BBC got near, but was still on the low side. David said that on the day the riots started, the BBC *Focus On Africa* reporters on the scene had been very accurate. Today, apart from the occasional car carrying Ibos back home, the city feels quiet. But the Christians have sent their families home in droves. The fathers stay behind in their jobs waiting to see what turns up.

In true Nigerian manner, many are called but few arrive at a Chinese restaurant that evening, the second biggest in Africa after Jo'burg. The reasons for this odd state of affairs is hard to pin down. But the guests, three from the *Triumph* and one from Kano Radio, are good value. I ask them which of Nigeria's rulers they rate highest? The first says that he rates Obasanjo. He had not thought so until he had taken part in a conference at Obasanjo's farm. He emerged impressed by the man's generosity of spirit and genuine breadth of mind. He rated him a big figure. The second said that Balewa, the first civilian ruler, was his choice. He was filled with the spirit of decency and tried to set the country on a sound course. The third chose Gowon because of the way he reconciled the nation with his "no victors, no vanquished" policy. The fourth paused and said: "I will tell you who is the worst – Babangida".

There was talk of the clandestine hand of the old politicians in the transition to democracy. I asked what they could say about this? They said everyone knew it was going on, it could be referred to in general terms, but they could not possibly accuse someone of breaking the law by taking part in politics when they were banned. The SDP had just had a re-run of one of its disputed gubernatorial contests. The result was out that evening and to their evident delight, the original winner had won the re-run to the discomfiture of the party managers. What did they think of the "open ballot" system? All four said it was a nonsense and could not work, certainly could not achieve what it was supposed to do.

In the cool evening, with a crescent moon half full, lying on its back, the air still smells of the smoky pungency of the desert. David shows me how to close various security doors in the house around my bedroom "in case dee teef man he cum in dee nite". He does not.

Thursday 14 November. The Emir of Kano is in London so he cannot receive me. Pity – it is apparently a very grand experience. But his Secretary shows us round the palace and the main receiving rooms, medium size chambers with vaulted roofs – mud vaulting? – decorated in mainly abstract patterns in grey, silver and dark brown. They are bold rather than crude and have a distinctive character of their own. The height of the ceiling and the intensity of the decoration hit you as you come in through the doorway, a clever piece of drama which puts the visitor in his place. Palace guards are magnificent in their flowing red and green gowns. Green sets off a black face dramatically.

Fenella and I leave to reach Jaji, the Military Staff and Command College, by 1 pm. They have rescheduled their day in order to fit me in. The Kano-Kaduna road is new, fast and dual carriageway so we make it in good time. In fact, instructed to arrive at 1300 we reach the Commandant's Office at precisely 1301. The Commandant of what he proudly calls a "Command and Staff College", not a mere Staff College, is General Haladu. He is big but not fat with strong handsome features, a strong baritone voice, speaks excellent unaccented English and was clearly highly intelligent. He spent a year at Aberystwyth reading international relations. Perish the thought, I can see his face peering from some more elevated presidential portrait in a few years time.

The entire course of, say, 250 majors and equivalents are gathered in the lecture hall. I decide that my Lagos speech is not suitable and instead talk in off the cuff terms about the things needed to create a free media: the responsibilities, personal, professional and institutional of journalists; and then regale them with tales of countries which have gagged their media and found total ruin at the end of the road.

I talk for thirty minutes, leaving them forty-five for questions. While some of their themes are by now predictable, they come from the standpoint of soldiers and not professional journalists. I say that I want to hear their views about the role of the media. Four hands go up, evidently eager to reply, but I have left it too late. The chairman announces "Commandant Sir, wishes to put a question." Commandant Sir has, I decide, taken the view that either he does not want this kind of debate, or does not think it suitable. He makes it clear that his question is designed to subsume the answers to my question. It was very elegant, and a stylish shutout of my attempt at debate which I could only admire.

Was it worth it? Yes, though I could not divine for a moment what the mood of this student body was on this crucial issue. I can only hope that the odd word or phrase will have resonated with someone who might have to take decisions about the media in the future. In general, the chattering public has these views about the military: (a) universal, the military must go. (b) very divided, the military want to go, or the military have created a transition process to democracy so chaotic that it is intended not to succeed. (c) well known, that staff college gameplans –academic of course – are examining the fourth republic. (d) universal, that if the military do leave and civilians do take over, then this time the military must let the civilians make at least one mess and get out of it themselves.

Nigeria's civil culture has never had long enough to establish itself through trial and error. All there has been has been the errors, followed by the trials. Fenella is under strict instructions from Jim to despatch me by 3.30 so that I am in Abuja by nightfall.

The horrors of Nigerian roads by dark are only hinted at. I set off with Bowa, a Council driver of quite exceptional patience, stamina and skill. The great Nigerian road through the flat, dusty north is timeless. Strings of white, large-horned Fulani cattle and their herdsmen are moving to the better pastures. The occasional water holes still have water in them after the season's good rains. Reed beds of great bushy reeds come and go.

Outside Kaduna, the new dual highway is being built on the left of the existing road. Thirty kilometres further on, the new road coming up from Abuja suddenly materialises on the right. Fifty kilometres later it is back to the left. Does anyone know what is going on? Meanwhile the surface of the existing road has rather given up the ghost. It is pock-marked with pot holes, eroded surfaces, causing the traffic to weave drunkenly from side to side so that sometimes the right is on the left and the left is on the right until they regain their correct positions just in time. At other times, the road is a confusion of every imaginable means of communication, with cars, lorries, buses, vans, pedestrians, wheel barrows weaving in and out in a chaotic order.

The light falls as we turn onto the new twin track highway to the hand-built federal capital of Abuja. The Hilton stands like a vast irrelevance in the acres of building sites. Its decor is amazing. It is exactly like the Hilton in Geneva, all mirrors and pink plastic panelling. The sense of isolation is matched only by the sense of relief. The telephones get to London in 30 seconds.

Friday November 15. Leave hotel at 7.30 for an early start on the Shell private Twin Otter taking me, Jim Whittell and the Shell Director of Government and Public Affairs, Chris Folaria Williams, down to the oil fields. It is a 100 minute flight over green hills and occsional fields and cultivation. Once the Niger slid into view, massive with its islands like irrelevant obstructions to the huge flow of the water. From time to time I feel that the energetic clearing and cultivation is about to destroy the tropical forest, at others it looks as if the clearings are merely nibbling at the fringes of nature.

We land at the Shell refinery at Warri, on a short strip which has to close the road along its end when a plane is taking off or landing. A hectic day long tour of Shell's projects – a model farm to help local farmers improve their crop yields; a development well where the drilling and associated work have just ended and the site will be cleared of equipment leaving only a "Christmas tree" and some piping behind. A blocked road delays us by putting 20 kilometres onto our journey to the well. We have only just asked the basic questions when a Bristow Bell helicopter thumps overhead for the next leg of the day – a flight across the delta to the Forcados Terminal, where all the oil in the area is gathered before being treated and pumped out to the ocean single buoy terminals.

The delta is unbelievably beautiful, the arms of the river seeming to lie stationary like solid brown toffee. As they gather strength and meet the main stream of the river, its sheer size drives the inconceivable volume of water down to the sea in a clearly visible and rapid curent. From the canopy of foliage, the occasional flame tree breaks through. Elsewhere the canopy gives way to bare, unrelieved mangrove swamp. From time to time a cluster of palm-thatched huts mark a fishing village, accessible only by water, assuming that anybody can find it. "What do you think that the open ballot or the census mean to these people?" someone asks.

Saturday 18 November. Last business date – a sixty-minute phone-in live on Federal Radio. These broadcasters fly by the seat of their pants. Just three lines, one for Lagos and two for the rest of the country, all routed through one multi-source telephone. There are times in the first five minutes when I wonder if anyone will phone in, but then it gets going and is going strong until the end.

Some callers are very generous in their praise. One misses the demise of *Songs of Praise*. Others voice the by now customary doubts. One is very passionate. Another asks for news of Jack de Manio and Alyn Aynsworth. The most acute points out that although no one responsible is really asking for the news not to be reported, they are asking for more than those minimal, harsh facts. I say that in the end they are simply asking too much of us. Until there is a bigger, sounder, better local media environment they will continue to have expectations of us which we cannot fully meet.

This is I believe the last word. What are my last thoughts at the end of this week of ceaseless talk about the media in general and our role in particular? First, that we broadcast more about Africa than anybody else. Second, that we provide more information about Africa than anybody else. Third, that the coverage – from news to drama – is exceptionally wide. Fourth, that everybody including the critics knows this. Their expectations are, however, larger. Listeners want to be reassured, they want to know that an organisation on which they rely so much, should love and support them too. They are hurt by the truth about their continent, a truth with which they have to live every day of their lives. "Respect Africa" is a line in a pop song about African football. Too often, our reporting of criticism, of failure, strikes home as a lack of respect. That is not why we do it; but I can certainly understand that that is how it often feels.

Written during a visit to Nigeria, November 10–18 1991.

CHAPTER 10
SOUND AND VISION

W HEN MARK ANTONY addressed the Roman crowd after the murder of Julius Caesar at the Capitol on the Ides of March, he began his speech by saying: "Friends, Romans, countrymen, lend me your ears". We can only applaud. Mark Antony was clearly a man of the radio. He was not the first. The oral tradition in Greece which probably accounts for the creation of the Odyssey and the Iliad totally relied on the power of the word as a powerful instrument of communication – the most powerful. One thousand years after Homer, St. John begins his Gospel with the statement, "In the beginning was the Word", and one of the most powerful injunctions in the Gospels is "He that hath ears to hear, let him hear".

These are reminders to us, people of the air, that radio links the audience to the broadcasters in the most time-honoured way – through the ear. Audiences still listen. Despite the atrophying effect of too much exposure to television, the listening organ has not withered away in a twist of Darwinian evolution. When audiences tire of the banality of images on television, what do they do – they turn away from the picture but leave the sound on. The ear has won over the eye.

It may seem that radio lent the ears of our listeners to television on temporary extended loan – it may have even surrendered them too easily – but the evidence exists that radio is not a thing of the past. In 1919, the American writer Lincoln Steffens told Bernard Baruch, after a visit to the Soviet Union,"I have seen the future and it works". The trouble was that he looked and did not listen.

In the interests of accuracy, I should say that what Lincoln Steffens said to Baruch was "I have been over into the future and it works". This is an example of what we can call the Danforth Quayle effect – a person is credited with a remark that they either did not make at all – the Super-Quayle – or not in the form in which history has chosen to pass it on. History is a ruthless sub-editor and often a good one. I am sure Steffens would have said what he is now credited with saying, had he thought it was going down into the Book of Quotations.

Had he listened would he have been able to reach the same conclusion? The television viewer in the Soviet Union, like the television camera, had to endure exposure to official images, officially presented. For years it was impossible to look behind the official facade. In the eighteenth century, Potemkin, the lover of Catherine II, and then a powerful regional governor, was credited with the ruse that convinced the Empress that all was well with her empire. As she toured the country, Potemkin built a series of villages made only of wooden facades. They were then dismantled and put up at the next site once the Empress had moved on. When Hollywood built its sets they were building on the experience of Potemkin. As he fooled Catherine into believing that the nation was prosperous, so did Hollywood fool the millions. The stratagem was simple, but it fools too many of the people, too much of the time.

Television cameras can't look round the corner especially if there is a burly militia man, or an assiduous Ministry minder barring the way. The eye can be fooled by the image of the surface. The mind is more critical. The ear can hear the creaking of the wooden supports behind the facade, tell-tale creaking which says that all is not as it appears to be.

Ten years ago, I made a series of television reports from the Soviet Union. Those were the days of Brezhnevian stagnation. The dead hand of official information policy lay over our every movement. Its guiding principle appeared to be "if it moves, don't shoot it". But if it was stationary, such as a bridge, a pylon, a road, then it was strategic and secret and you certainly could not shoot it. We were led to a series of officially chosen locations where entirely happy Soviet citizens were engaged in entirely satisfying activities in an entirely perfect environment. We had no alternative but to shoot what we were shown. Only on our return to London did the solution suggest itself. It was to cut the film absolutely straight – what we saw was what we showed. But the commentary explained that this was all that we were allowed to show, and it contrasted the official picture with what was left out and with what we knew from other sources. The word told the eye that it was watching a series of Potemkin locations. Left to itself, the eye would have been a victim of manipulation. But the mind and the ear supplied the information which could make sense of the evidence.

I hope that I have not been too fanciful in emphasising my belief that, despite having worked in television and being a great admirer of it, radio has both a fine past and a great future. Why does it have a great future? Because radio set ownership is on the increase. It stands at present at 2,037 million, which is very nearly one for every other person on the planet. This figure has doubled since 1975. High as it is, there is still a very long way to go before saturation is reached. I do not know about anyone else, but I own nine assorted radio sets, which distorts the gross figures somewhat. My colleague who runs the BBC domestic radio possesses twenty.

Actual radio ownership is a mere one per nine people in sub-Saharan Africa and one per ten people in India. But these areas are already recording very high rates of increase in ownership. Radio set ownership has trebled in India and sub-Saharan Africa since 1975 and increased in China by a factor of 8, reflecting the big advance in rural incomes and standards of living since 1979. The desire to own a radio set is high – it remains the most desired consumer durable. In India, even the very poor want one, and many buy one. Thirty per cent of the Indian population are classified as living below the poverty line, that is to say consuming less than US $11 per month. Yet the bottom 60% of the population bought one third of the radios sold in India. Some of those purchasers must have been very poor indeed.

Of course there is a huge demand for television. Starting from very low bases, tv ownership in China has increased since 1975 by a factor of 200, in India by a factor of 60, in Africa by 70. Yet there are still fewer than half as many tv sets in ownership as there are radios. We are still in big business.

What makes these people listen? Here, I draw my conclusions principally from our experience as international broadcasters, though many of the reasons given may also apply to domestic broadcasters and audiences in the United States. Firstly, because they need to know, and therefore they have to listen. Knowledge is a matter of life or death; continuous information about events keeps hope alive. Secondly, because the local media can't give a full or accurate picture of events, or, more commonly, because they peddle a party line which bears only a passing relationship to the truth. It was always difficult to imagine living in an environment where the information media suppressed the truth and banned discussion of certain subjects. In the Socialist bloc, unemployment could not be an issue because, objectively, it did not exist. Pollution was not a subject to be reported because, objectively, it could not exist in a socialised economy. What then did an unemployed or under-employed worker in a deeply polluted part of Poland feel? No wonder they turned to the international radios.

Thirdly, people listen because local media give only a very fragmentary picture of events. They do not so much distort by design, as by omission, by incompleteness, by under-playing the significance of events or their seriousness, and by underestimating the intelligence of their audience. I wonder whether much of that does not also apply to the commercial part of American radio – perhaps the difference between public radio broadcasters and those from commercial radio does not lie so much in the way public affairs are addressed. The very diversity and diversification of American commercial radio creates an information environment where the listening public is starved of a full picture of national and international events. I call it technological deprivation.

Niche broadcasting is all very well and it clearly does very well for those who define the niche. What does it do for the citizen? It segments the nation into the minutest fragments of geographical separation, musical interest, intellectual taste, age group and economic buying power. In this view of life, nobody can be a citizen with a national and international interest, or can refuse to exist in pre-determined market categories. Such an approach fragments national identity without creating local awareness, reduces what people share and have in common and emphasises what sets them apart. Technology deprives them, by its facility, by its apparent variety, of a unifying experience. If this description of an audience such as the United States is true, then these audiences "need to know" almost as much as the more obviously deprived audiences behind the Iron Curtain.

How much evidence is there that audiences can be driven by a real, acute and measurable need to know? Recent research during and after the Gulf War points strongly to the conclusion that they do. In the United Kingdom, the main BBC speech network, Radio 4, devoted one of its frequencies – the national FM frequency – to continuous news coverage of events in the Gulf Crisis. One and a half million extra listeners tuned in as a result. Seventy per cent of these listeners were aged between 16 and 44. Ninety-one percent were in the ABC social classes. These audiences not only grew, they listened to more hours of radio during the crisis. Radio 4 FM, or "Scud FM" as it became known, sometimes affectionately, sometimes less so, met a real audience need. This evidence is confirmed by research in other countries. In France, the news information station, France Info, recorded a doubling of its daily audience during the Gulf War period. In the Netherlands, listening at the start of the crisis was up by 25% over the same time a year ago. We know from the experience of many affiliates in the United States how much audiences there wanted authoritative analysis of that complex crisis, and we were delighted when so many Americans turned to the World Service as the supplier of that material. World Service research in the Middle East during the Gulf Crisis showed that listening – in Arabic – had almost doubled at this time.

The conclusion I draw from the Gulf experience is this, and it rests on no scientific analysis whatever. Television, and to a lesser extent radio, has finally created the global village of awareness of events in the remotest parts of the globe. Neville Chamberlain's infamous throw-away about Czechoslovakia in 1938: "a quarrel in a far-away country between people of whom we know nothing" is not politically possible today or permissible morally. But the global village of awareness also possesses other, less desirable features: it is a global village of frustration and impotence at our inability to do much about the horrors that fill our screens; and it is a global village with a desire for understanding. A viewer today might turn Chamberlain's remark on its head and lament about "far-away crises, about which we know too much, and about which we can do too little". Television by the power, immediacy and speed of its supply of images creates the awareness, but cannot supply the desire for understanding or meet the human need to connect knowledge with action.

Radio has the ability to meet those needs better than television. Could it be perhaps that television and radio are now entering a new symbiotic relationship, where each delivers in a complementary way, the information at which it excels? The need of the right hemisphere of the brain to meet the needs of intuition and feeling, we leave to television; satisfying the left hemisphere, the area of logic, languages and thought is the province of radio. Together they make up the balanced brain, the complete citizen. If this has any truth in it at all, then radio is not challenged by television. It is re-integrated into the national media pattern because of the desire of a significant part of the audience to have its perception of the public world re-integrated in this way.

How are we responding to this new situation, now that the experience of the Gulf War has brought thinking about radio news to a head? There have been several innovations and discoveries. As the coalition air forces struck into Kuwait and Iraq, the World Service, for the first time ever, turned itself into a rolling news and comment format. It was risky, and only stayed on air for the first few hours, but once established it ran with increasing authority during those early hours of the campaign.

The World Service also established an intensified pattern of news bulletins, usually containing correspondents' voice pieces. This break with sacred World Service news traditions – "if the news is the news, then it should come from a news reader" – should not be underestimated. It reflected our belief that to deny the listener the eye-witness account of the correspondent in their actual voice would have been to deny them a vital piece of information. Yet now that events are – by the standards of the height of the crisis – back to normal, we have retained some "illustrated news bulletins", while keeping at regular intervals throughout the 24 hours the classic World Service news format of the single-voiced bulletin.

An increased number of sixty-minute news and current affairs sequences were also carried. In the post-war scene, we now have at least one further edition of Newsdesk and one extra edition of Newshour – but that was planned long before. Undoubtedly, the war experience has hastened the tilt of our coverage towards more, extended and fuller news and current affairs throughout the 24-hour period. For the future, we will introduce a third edition of Newshour at 0500 GMT in early 1992. Longer term plans include two more editions before the end of 1993. If completed, the World Service will be a very different network from what it was even a year ago.

Why not go the whole hog and become a 24-hour news network? In Britain, many, and not just the broadcasters, think that is what the BBC should do both at home and on the World Service. Many listeners, though, do not, and we received a number of letters of protest from those who objected to the changes in schedule, or who thought that there was too much news coverage. I believe that what would be needed, if we went down this road, would be a network split, with one providing the hard, immediate news and

149

information, the other providing the drama, documentary and other entertainment aspects. There are many ways in which the hard news channel can develop. I am a critic of what I understand by "rolling news", which consists of a repetitive unit of 20-30 minutes taking a restricted view of the subjects the public wants to know about, limits the amount of time given to those subjects, and bores to death anyone who listens for more than the length of the basic unit.

If, under the impact of the lessons of the Gulf War, the World Service does become a news network – and I say if – it would need the following things: first, proper funding. Second, a further, separate network which would meet the huge demand for non-news information, entertainment and education that we carry at present. Third, a commitment to avoid the trap of narrow formatting and rigid time-constraints, and to give the listener both greater immediacy, greater understanding and a wider range of political debate on those issues. There is no point in extending the time given to news and then, in effect, reducing the quality and volume of information contained in the news by a limited format. That would be to give the listeners a rock instead of the loaf of bread.

I end with the question of words and images, the eye and the ear. Shakespeare knew the difference and the difficulty. We are all suggestible about what we see. Hamlet teases the old courtier, Polonius. He asks Polonius if he can see that cloud shaped like a camel? Polonius agrees that it is indeed very like a camel. Hamlet: "Methinks it is like a weasel?" Polonius: "It is back'd like a weasel". Hamlet: "Or like a whale?" Polonius: "Very like a whale". When it comes to images we are all easily manipulated and subjective. That is why images are so rich, because their shapes are so complex. On another occasion, Polonius tries to draw Hamlet into conversation. "What do you read, My Lord?" Hamlet replies: "Words, words, words".They didn't save him, but no-one can stop listening.

First delivered to the American Public Radio Conference in New Orleans, 17 May 1991.

CHAPTER 11
ANCIENT GODS
AND SACRED COWS

ANYBODY who accepts an invitation to talk about creative management has got beyond the stage of worrying about being considered presumptuous. False modesty is, on balance, an even less attractive characteristic than presumption. The latter at least involves taking risks in exposing ideas and views in public and the danger of intellectual rebuff and even demolition. Far better to put ideas of good manners behind us and go down the path of challenging assertion and readiness to face criticism in the process.

Let me take up the subject by addressing it in five stages. First, what were my assumptions before becoming Managing Director? Secondly, what did I learn between getting the job and starting work? Thirdly, what were my operating principles when I started? Fourthly, how were they put into practice? Fifthly, to the extent that they have been put into practice, can they be said to amount to creative management?

When I applied for the post of Managing Director of the BBC External Services in 1986, I had no managerial background or experience at all. For twenty-six years, I had worked as a journalist in radio and television. My responsibilities were to that activity alone – they were entirely professional and personal. If my application was to be successful, then I had to put forward some thoughts about aims and purposes – a "Vision" – and more detailed ideas about how they might be realised – a "Mission Statement". In 1986, I would not have recognised either a Vision or Mission Statement if they had walked through the door, but you do not have to have been to the London Business School to organise your ideas in this way. Business cant aside – that was to come much later – that is what I instinctively tried to do.

I submitted a two-and-a-half page note to the Board of Governors in advance of the interview. Only one paragraph relates directly to management – the rest was editorial and political – and this is what it said about the External Services:

> *The role of the Managing Director is to define and express the editorial basis of its broadcasts; to defend its independent voice in the interests of the British public, the listeners and existing and future governments; to argue the case for the maintenance and preferably the expansion of its services; to lead it into new areas offered by new technologies where its unique editorial authority can achieve further projection; to convince Bush House itself that a voice which is that of a giant abroad is not that of a pigmy at home.*

What I could not know, until my colleague John Davis pointed it out recently, was that these instincts fitted in well with definitions of management leadership given by Goldsmith and Clutterbuck, in *The Winning Streak*: He provided me with this quotation from that book:

> *Leaders are visible; leaders provide a clear mission, which they believe in passionately themselves and incite others to subscribe to; and leadership thrives where people have clear objectives and the resources to strike out for them.*

Right or wrong in theoretical terms, my own definition was the best I could do. It was all right so far as it went, indeed wholly unexceptionable, and it had the merit of at least defining the MD's role as editorial, strategic, innovative and very public.

The notes I made preparing for the interview were rather fuller, though I cannot recall how far what I sketched out on paper influenced what I said in the course of the sixty-minute interview. "What Needs Doing?" I wrote boldly, in the best Leninist fashion. Editorial and journalistic approaches have got rather "stuck in the mud. Programmes are now very old ... I get the impression that a little spring cleaning is overdue." I noted that the margin between what was safe journalistically and what was new had to be examined. "I think it is very easy to get complacent and say 'we have the finest news-gathering machine' and never ask 'why are we so seldom first with the news?' Because if you are that good you should be first some of the time."

Next, the relationship between Bush House and its domestic cousins needed attention. Thinking in 1986, it seemed to me that "Bush tends to be rather exclusive, rather intolerant of the more brash news palette of its domestic sisters – it tends to flinch at the mention of television." (This was particularly unfair since the outgoing MD, Austen Kark, had just started a joint project with BBC TV under Bill Cotton to develop a pilot for a World Television News Service in March 1986.) My conclusion was that "Bush needs jolting out of its morbid isolation".

Again, such observations were easy enough to make, but hardly added up to a serious philosophy of management. At the very end of my notes, and not before time, I steeled myself to explain to the Governors why someone without any management experience should be trusted with such management responsibility? I argued first that broadcasters are not merely remote, unaware figures concerned only with cameras or microphones.

> Broadcasters have a very direct awareness of management because they are at the receiving end of it - this obliges them to look critically at the decisions that are made which affect their working lives … I have been at the receiving end of quite a number of decisions, some of which were a good deal better than others, and some of which were proved by time to be as bad as we said they were at the time.

Finally, there was a more general thought which sprang from discussions I had over previous years with two members of Mrs. Thatcher's first Think Tank, Norman Strauss and John Hoskyns. We need more "inners and outers" in management and the civil service, as on the American model.

> It is not the case that those who have been in the management system for fifteen years manage it better, all they do is manage it in the same way. It is not the case that outsiders cannot manage because they don't know the system, any system can be learned, the problem is to run that system in a new way appropriate to changing – in External Broadcasting's case – radically changing circumstances.

153

Whether such thoughts were material in influencing the Governors' decision, I carried them with me when I returned to Bush House. I was fortunate in asking for and getting three months' familiarisation with the External Services before taking over. In that time, I visted and talked to every departmental head, and every one of the 37 language section heads.

At the end of these meetings, a number of strong impressions had formed and at a comparatively early stage, each succeeding interview tended to confirm the broad picture that was already taking shape. First, it was an organisation which had been under financial, economic, political and institutional pressure for so long that everybody was simply and understandably shellshocked. As a result, the main management characteristic was one of response to events, the expected norm being that something bad was about to occur, with reality currently being pretty obliging in living up to such pessimistic expectations.

The inevitable consequences were low expectations that anything would get better; and widespread frustration that scores of good ideas could not be put into practice. Bush House's capacity to endure government cuts, and worse still seemingly persistent government inquiries – about one every four to five years – was heroic. But no institution in such a situation and frame of mind could start to take the initiative or seek to become master of its own destiny.

By September 1986, when I became Managing Director, I knew that there were five broad aims which needed achieving. First, energies had to be released and frustrations eased. In many cases, all it required was to say "yes" to a good idea. Even this was mildly shocking since events had made "no" the more usual response. People had to be given the confidence to act on their own good ideas. Secondly, a number of people in important middling positions had to be encouraged to leave – decently and in their own time. They were congenital "no" sayers and would or could never change. In their place, outsiders with new ideas and without the bureaucratic battle scars of a decade and a half were needed. Thirdly, Bush House needed telling internally that it was good. Fourthly, insiders needed to see that the outside world was being

154

told that they were good. It became a policy, for instance, to reply to critical comments or letters in the press fast and robustly. Finally, money had to be found to make the process of "saying yes" a reality for those projects where a good idea was not enough by itself. We had to overcome what I called Bush House's "psychosis of poverty".

I was reasonably confident that such a five-point approach was not a private one but was consonant with the lessons gleaned from three months' intensive talking to middle and senior management. I was not to know – until my colleague John Davis pointed it out – that these five principles bore a reassuring resemblance to the "classical" approach to administration set out by Henri Fayol in his study of the French mining industry in 1947. These were: "To forecast and plan; to organise – build up the structure, material and human, of the undertaking; to command; to co-ordinate – binding together, unifying and harmonizing all activity and effort; to control – seeing that everything occurs in conformity with established rule". These five principles, however expressed, now had to be turned into actual policies.

The first consideration was the actual matter of leadership style. I did not have to choose one; there was only one of which I was capable – public, visible, accessible. A former colleage, now a subordinate, said cheerfully: "It won't last; they'll have you stuck in your office within a year". Two years later he had the generosity to admit that he had been wrong. Another colleage returned from a Cabinet Office course with the news that the greatest management insight had been the importance of "MBWA": "Management by Walking Around". Having morning coffee or lunch in the canteen is not only pleasant – I have been doing it off and on for thirty-one years in that essential basement nerve-centre of Bush House – it is highly effective, and saves a huge amount of time. Much business is transacted by running across people, with whom a formal meeting would otherwise have to be arranged, blocking up an already full diary.

Then there was the question of the leadership tone of Bush House's senior managers. They were able, dedicated, experienced, devoted, but were quite extraordinarily introverted as a group. I told them as much, and they took no offence. Years later, a close

155

colleague said: "To be a good manager, you have to be an optimist". He was right. What I was saying to my colleagues about their collective introversion was that we all had to adopt a management style among ourselves and towards the organisation which indicated that we believed that things could get better. Not appearing too introverted was an essential part of the process of changing the stance adopted by management in its work, towards the staff, and towards the world outside.

Something else needed putting in place. Many external influences bore down on us, urging us, pushing us in the direction that we went; from Whitehall, in the guise of the Financial Management Initiative, and later, of the Next Steps philosophy; from the BBC corporately, which was introducing 250 of its senior staff to Performance Management. For our part, we developed a growing body of management experience and philosophy among the dozen of us who have run Bush House in recent years. We discovered a healthy two-way process; certain things that we did were validated by management theory; we did other things because we were introduced to them by management theory. Together, they created a healthy interaction between principle and practice which kept both of them alive.

At this early and crucial stage, a big but difficult opportunity arose. The 1985 Perry Report – initiated by the Treasury – had recommended that External Broadcasting should be funded on a Triennial basis, thus removing the deadly, sapping annual bureaucratic struggle for public money. In the autumn of 1986, the first glimpse of a slight easing of the financial strait jacket appeared in our budgets. It would be possible to fund some new ideas, to begin the process of innovation and stimulation, to attack that very "psychosis of poverty" which afflicted External Broadcasting's thinking and approach. But Perry also set us a challenge, to establish an entirely new, ground up, priority-based budgeting system. Since Perry did not elaborate exactly how it should work, we asked the BBC's auditors, Deloitte Haskins Sells, who had had a representative on the Perry Committee, to devise a system for us. It involved a departmental review of activities set against objectives with allocation of budgets against those activities. Finally, every department had to offer 5% of its budget as savings, these savings being graded in order of pain and acceptability by the senior managers. The cumulated savings could then be put towards the many bids for new or enhanced activities.

What matters is not whether this was or is novel or banal. It was wholly new at Bush House. While everybody recognised that it would have to be introduced sooner or later, many argued that the acquisition of new skills, the change of culture and approach were so revolutionary that the system could only be fully introduced in January 1988, that is in the next budget round but one. Others, including myself, believed that change once identified could not be deferred with any justification. We would not look serious if we delayed or prevaricated. We decided to put it into operation immediately, within three months.

This was the single most important decision affecting Bush House in the last six years. It had the following consequences: through the forced identification of savings, for the first time we generated money for allocation to our priority activities without constant resort to Whitehall; learning the budget process started an entire managerial revolution, as a result of which the old dichotomy between editors and managers started to breakdown – good editors soon became the better managers. It initiated a process of identifying unnecessary spending in areas where previously we had lacked the tools to search for it; we began to feel independent in our actions because we created room for manoeuvre each year where we believed it to be needed. In short, this single decision – questioned, complained about, but not ultimately resisted – was the key that unlocked the door to a degree of managerial freedom which began to match the editorial independence External Broadcasting had always had. Traditional editorial freedom was to be hugely and properly bolstered by a greater degree of managerial flexibility.

Finally, no Whitehall bureaucrat could complain of this new conjunction of forces – we were only implementing and operating the recommendations of a committee which the bureaucrats themselves had set up. Three years on, the substantial productivity and efficiency gains which Bush House could demonstrate in the documentation for the next Triennial Grant-in-Aid were a convincing part of the argument leading ultimately to a real increase in funding for the years 1991-4.

Let us retrace our steps to 1986-7. Within the first year, two innovative editorial processes also began. They signalled unequivocally that review and change were expected, that standing pat on the status quo was not a luxury that could be defended, still less afforded. As John Harvey-Jones has observed: "To move forward, you have to make the status quo uncomfortable".

The first was World Service Renewal, a root and branch review of the output of the English language network by small teams drawn from all over Bush House. Masterminded by the network's editor, Anthony Rendell, it confirmed my earlier impression that ideas and energy, latent and plentiful, were waiting to erupt, given the chance. The teams generated ideas from which Rendell was later able to draw up a "Red Book" of reform of the network, most of whose ideas have now been implemented. Most importantly, there is no danger of the network slipping back into immobilism – another World Service Renewal programme should not be necessary because it is renewing itself the whole time.

What Anthony Rendell did has been well summed up by Peter Drucker: "The manager has the task of creating a true whole that is larger than the sum of the parts, a productive entity that turns out more than the sum of the resources put into it". This was particularly true: Rendell had to re-shape the network with minimal extra resources; change had to come from ideas, from people, it could not be achieved by throwing money around – money which was not even there.

The second editorial initiative related to the 37 other languages. Senior managers, including the Managing Director, had no direct idea of what the vernaculars – as they were called – were broadcasting or how they were broadcasting. Much of the actual material was, of course, centrally produced, such as the news and many analytical talks. This fact hardly seemed adequate as a substitute for serious direct editorial control and my predecessor, Austen Kark, pointed me strongly towards the need for action in that area.

After some study, a system called Programme Evaluation was developed under which a panel of twelve from all over Bush House would examine the recorded output of three days of a language service at a time, comparing the output with back translations of the broadcasts.

The scheme produced real resistance. It was unnecessary – it was said – it discriminated against the language services, it was a rough and ready tool, it would give only a partial picture, it would lead to people unversed in the nuances of other languages and cultures passing crude judgements on complex editorial matters – in other words, it drew a chorus of special pleading. The process of change was introduced with some public pain and rather more private anguish in those sections who first fell under scrutiny, and involved – in management-speak – "coercion": it had to happen.

Five years on, it has become part of the editorial landscape. Editorial review is undertaken by Controllers on a continuing basis; the Newsroom has begun its own reviews of its output with its customers, the language services, an idea that would once have been regarded as demeaning, unnecessary and almost heretical. Programme evaluation review is, in short, now part of the accepted processes of the World Service. It has also contributed to a far wider knowledge of the problems and achievements of the language services; it has broken down internal barriers, removed misconceptions, and evened up editorial standards by making clear that editorial standards were themselves to be commonly applied. To borrow the language of management again, the change has now been "internalised".

Taken together, these three early initiatives – the new budgeting system, World Service Renewal, Programme Evaluation – added up to a powerful signal that change was needed, and that the rhetoric of change would lead to genuine alterations in management and broadcasting. Yet the rhetoric of change itself is not sufficient and the use of such rhetoric depends crucially on one factor. No institution can be transformed without respect for its values and its achievements. Even radical change has some of its roots in the institution as it exists at the time. Those who have worked in an institution for years and brought it to a high level of achievement and public esteem are hardly likely to respond to an instruction to change which implicitly or explicitly undermines or undervalues much of what they have been doing. An institution must be loved and respected if it is to be changed. Provided that such love and

159

respect exists, and its existence is recognised, then the process of change itself can be fairly brisk, not least because there will be people who wish to be part of it because it meets their own wishes. Without love and respect, a clamorous programme of change can only run into resistance, and never gain full intellectual legitimacy.

Management needs other characteristics, too, if it is to put such programmes into practice. First, a sense of danger. The ability to identify the issue that might lead to a major crisis cannot be over-estimated. The temptation is to ignore early warning signs because it is too much effort and it is easier to hope that they will blow over. They rarely do, and a rapid move to identify them as dangers which should be addressed and managed is the only prudent response. While the danger cannot always be eliminated, its effects can be diminished and the very process of tackling it gives the proper impression of an institution which is in charge of its affairs rather than an institution that is buffetted by events and circumstances. This sits well with the 1982 definition of a manager's function produced by Rosemary Stewart, that of being what she called a "Disturbance Handler": one who "resolves situations arising from unpredictable events beyond his or her control".

Secondly, a well-managed institution is a thinking institution. It thinks about its future. This has many advantages. It is enjoyable. It is fun, and man is after all Homo Ludens. It is also smart and helps you keep abreast of your enemies at least, and well ahead of them most of the time. The World Service has recently completed a process called simply "World Service 2000". For six months last year, nine strategy groups examined all the main programme, engineering and managerial activities with a view to identifying where we might be in 2000 and what we needed to do in the intervening period in order to get there. The groups were chosen from the senior and middle production levels, people in their 30s, without managerial experience for the most part. We sought the ideas of the next generation of middle and senior mangers.

The process has been very successful. It identified many things which needed doing now – they have already been adopted into the current managerial agenda. It also created a strong strategic agenda, whose communication to the whole institution will provide a great opportunity for positive internal reinforcement. And most interestingly, it introduced sixty able people to the sheer challenge of management planning. For the first time it dawned on them that there were some activities that were as rewarding and creative as making programmes. At the end of the process, they urged us to expose as many people as we could to such a task of analysis and creativity.

What kind of managers are we? Functionally, I recognise the definitions of Henry Mintzberg and Rosemary Stewart:

1. *managers do not work according to the neat well organised themes of the classical management school;*

2. *their activities are characterized by brevity, variety and fragmentation;*

3. *they spend most of their time interacting with other people rather than thinking well-organised thoughts;*

4. *they work at a brisk and continuing pace with little free time;*

5. *so far from being subject to extremely generalised comments about 'what all managers do' there is a substantial variety in the objective demands of managerial jobs.*

And where do we fit in psychologically as a management team of twelve? In his book *Inside Organisations* – so John Davis tells me – Charles Handy identifies four basic character approaches to management drawn from classical archetypes – the Zeus type, a man of impulse and lover of power; the Apollo type, the god of harmony, logic, and I'm afraid, of sheep. His followers like things tidy and ordered; the Athena type – excited by what is new. They like new problems and new situations. But they are also team people; and the Dionysiac – for whom quality is paramount, compromise is unacceptable, and dedication to craft overrides all.

Looking around at the dozen or so men and women who make up World Service's management team, I can easily recognise at least three Athena types, and three true Apollonians. I doubt if we have

a true Dionysiac, though we do care about standards. As for Zeus –
well, I cannot honestly recognise one, at least not in Handy's
definition. But then, probably I'm sitting in the wrong place to do
so.

First delivered to the "Account Planning Group" Annual Conference
on 14 May, 1992

CHAPTER 12
BOTTLED, CANNED OR LIVE?

I FELL IN LOVE with live broadcasting in October 1964. As a young producer in the then External Services, I was asked to chair the overnight extended rolling election coverage. It was a memorable twenty-four hours. The election was desperately close run – would the fourteenth Earl of Home, the man who did his economic calculations on the back of a matchbox, hold off the challenge of the white heat of the technological revolution held high by the fourteenth Harold Wilson? It was only late on the Friday afternoon that Harold Wilson was able to drive to the Palace to be asked to form the next government, with a towering majority of six.

Yet that was not all. In the late hours of election night, the Soviet Union's last reforming ruler before Mikhail Gorbachev, Nikita Sergeyevich Khrushchev, was overthrown. And for good measure, China – still led by Mao Tse Tung – exploded another nuclear device. In the last thirty minutes of transmission on the Friday afternoon, a small team of four who had born the brunt of the non-stop broadcasting burden, attempted to sum up the changes that had taken place so suddenly.

Because we had been talking for so long, because the issues had been raised randomly as they occurred, because the speakers had got used to one another, the discussion flowed with a coherence, cogency and economy that seemed exhilarating, illuminating and entertaining. Of course, we may all have been too tired to notice: I may be recalling it through rose-tinted earphones. Whether that particular broadcast was better or worse than I now remember, it left me with a strong preference for live broadcasting which has never left me and which experience has only confirmed.

Yet all broadcasters have many moments when they wish the microphones would go dead to cover their embarrassment. The last time this happened to me was during Radio Three's Weekend from the Twin Cities of Minneapolis and Saint Paul. After a particularly idiotic foul up over some linking material, I was walking back to the hotel before my next stint at the microphone and kicking myself for having made such a mistake. I decided that I had two choices; either I could immediately throw myself off the top of the Radisson Saint Paul Hotel; or I could forget all about it and continue the programme. I decided, of course, that there are worse things in life than daubing your face with scrambled egg on air. Live broadcasting is worth the risks, at least from this broadcaster's point of view. It is stimulating; it is danger-ous; it is direct; it imposes discipline on all those taking part; it is more lively to do; overall, in the area of news and analysis, it leads to a better result.

From the audience's point of view, who would have missed the start of the BBC *Six O'Clock News* on 20th November 1990, as John Sergeant was telling the British public that Mrs Thatcher was inside the British Embassy in Paris talking to her advisers, while the tv cameras showed her flanked by the armoured division of Bernard Ingham and storming down the steps of that very embassy to announce to a microphone commandeered from John Sergeant by Bernard Ingham that she would fight on; and who did not sense that the reckless, characteristic defiance of the statement held the seeds of her destruction in it?

Who would have missed Mikhail Gorbachev's news conference on his return from his Crimean detention, or the humiliation forced on him the next day by Boris Yeltsin when he finally visited the Russian Parliament to say 'thank you' for their steadfastness during the coup attempt, only to have a decree abolishing the Communist Party in the Russian Federation thrust in front of him for enforced signature? Power visibly passed at that moment. (One shouldn't forget, though, that the most revealing insights into the Soviet Revolution of 1991 came in a documentary series, Brian

Lapping and Norma Percy's *The Second Russian Revolution* – the very antithesis of the drive to live broadcasting that is under discussion here. But it is axiomatic for me that the desired end is to bring the best witness of events to the audience in the most appropriate way. In considering events after they have happened, the extended recording may be the best vehicle.)

Who would have missed that moment on *Newsnight* as the two Germanys were united? Huge celebrations, speeches, bands and fireworks were erupting all around the Brandenburg Gate, and Charles Wheeler had been condemned – with the best of editorial intentions – to be part of a live discussion with some immensely serious Germans about this great moment in modern history. When Jeremy Paxman, who was conducting the discussion, asked him what he thought of the event, Charles turned to camera and said with the authority available only to a journalist who had fought in the victory over Germany in 1945, "It's pure Monty Python, Jeremy, doing a discussion in the middle of a firework display". It was of course the last remark that anybody could have expected. It was a gloriously apt, relevant, percipient remark. Had it been a recording, you can bet that it would have been edited out. But Charles Wheeler's apparently anarchic comments sprang very properly from the nature of the broadcast itself. On one side, the semi-organised disorder of the events surrounding the moment of unification at the Brandenburg Gate; on the other, the very structured nature of the programme format itself. It was, understandably, attempting to put meaning and order onto the events, order which they declined to accept, and which Charles Wheeler's remark finally acknowledged.

To say that is not to criticise the programme; it is to suggest that meaning can come from surprising directions, and that on this occasion it came from a conjuction of a live event, jarringly counterpointed by rational analysis, synthesised by a professional, experienced correspondent.

For the first generation of radio broadcasters, there was only one form of broadcasting: live. It was both a matter of outlook and later a question of available technology. Reith – according to Frank Gillard – used to call recording "a fraud on the listener" and was opposed to it. But then Reith was a live and very present broadcasting part of the personality of the British Broadcasting Company. In his Diaries, Reith records how he was broadcasting the lunch-time news on the tenth day of the General Strike in 1926. In the middle of the bulletin he was told that Downing Street wanted him urgently on the phone. Reith told the listeners he was stopping there to get more important news, to return a few minutes later with the report that TUC leaders had visited the Prime Minister and were calling off the Strike forthwith. Reith records disarmingly: "It was rather wonderful to have been the first to give the news... It is great fun running a crisis".

The taste for presiding over the great moments of history did not leave him. When King Edward VIII was to broadcast news of his abdication to the world, Reith revelled in the thought that as he introduced the broadcast, his voice "would carry to the ends of the earth". Having uttered the fateful words: "This is Windsor Castle. His Royal Highness the Prince Edward", Reith records how the trivia of live broadcasting can sometimes threaten to obscure the main event. In his own account, once Reith had made the announcement, he was to slip out of the one chair facing the microphone to the left, while the Prince would slip in from the right. Tables being what they are, the abdicating monarch gave the table leg a resounding kick as he slipped in, very audibly transmitted to the listening multitudes. Subsequently, Reith was asked to confirm or deny a report that he had left the room after making the announcement, and had he then slammed the door in disgust? In his own account, he recalled: "It was even suggested that, by so doing, I was not forgetful of microphone sensitivity, but was indicating disapproval of what was to follow. I had left the room, but no microphone would have noted it." That story is a reminder of the fact that no one can determine the precise message that the whole audience will draw from a live broadcast.

During the 1930s, technology began to make radio recording a possibility. The Blattnerphone – electro-magnetic recording on steel tape – first captured speech in 1924. The BBC installed a Blattnerphone in 1930 and in November of that year used it to record George Vs speech at the opening of the India Round Table Conference. By 1932, the BBC Empire Service – forerunner of today's World Service – was using what were called then "bottled programmes" in order to meet the needs of broadcasting to five different time zones around the world. In 1935, the modern radio era began to take recognisable form with the introduction of MSS recorders – Marguerite Sound Studios – which used metal discs coated in lacquer, the sound being registered in grooves cut in the lacquer. The displaced curls of lacquer enjoyed the name of "swarf".

But there was real resistance to the idea of recording. J B Clark, Director of the Empire Service in 1938, expressed a widespread unease: "We still cannot feel that recording is as good and reliable as a live performance". Asa Briggs records that during this time, "live broadcasting was greatly preferred, almost on moral grounds, to recorded broadcasting: it suggested to the listener, this is it". And Briggs quotes a BBC official commenting: "If artists know they are being recorded and a re-take can be made if they 'fluff', they tend to give a mediocre performance".

Yet such attitudes were to be made irrelevant by history and by the steady march of technology. The first portable disc-recorder – the Riverside Portable, weighing in at a mere 35 lbs – was developed in 1943. Wynford Vaughan Thomas used it historically in action during the Anzio landings in January 1944. Recording could bring immediacy to events, it allowed broadcasts to break out of the confines of the studio. The war also demonstrated that in this field, as in so many others, the Germans were technically ahead. Staff at BBC Monitoring – according to Asa Briggs – had noted that the Germans knew how to cut and piece together "record strips like films", and had pointed to "possibilities of superimposing sound effects, of editing in general and faking in particular". In liberated Norway, Geoffrey Bridson, one of the fathers of radio drama features, came across a commandeered

German truck with Magnetaphon equipment in it. He immediately realised how outclassed, cumbersome, and obsolete all other mobile recording systems were.

It was a decade before EMI came up with a British portable tape recorder – the misnamed "midget", weighing a lively 16lbs – in 1952. Eight years later, when I first met it, it had a frequent tendency to break down, a poor microphone, and each recorded tape had to be rewound by hand. It was the smaller, lighter, more reliable, German-made Uher in the 1960s that finally made outside portable recording a pleasure rather than a constant tussle with a temperamental, unreliable and overweight beast. With such technical facility finally available, radio recording – whether studio based or portable – swept through broadcasting unstoppably.

While the outside recording gave producers the chance to bring to the audience an entirely new ingredient – the actuality of real citizens, of real people, of real experience – the sheer facility of recording began to take over life in the studios as well. Rayner Heppenstall, another of the pioneers of radio features, says in his memoir *Portrait of the Artist as a Professional Man* that the last time he did a live drama production was in 1957 – of Muriel Spark's *The Party Through the Wall*. Thereafter tape-recording, and editing of studio based programmes, became well-nigh universal. Heppenstall noted that even a studio-based discussion such as *The Critics* never required fewer than one hundred edits. Clearly, recording – originally a way of bringing actuality into the studio and of enlivening the raw material on which broadcasting was based – had turned into something different. It was the broadcasters' equivalent of packaged food, which is perhaps why recordings ceased being referred to as "bottled" and became "canned" instead. In 1960, about half the programmes for domestic radio were still broadcast live. By 1972, a BBC Publication noted that almost everything – including the inserts into live current affairs programmes – was recorded.

What was the outlook behind these practices? It consisted of an obsession with neatness and order, with controllability, with packaging, with fitting everything into precise time parcels. None of these are wrong or reprehensible in themselves. There was, too, an idealistic, strongly educational element behind them – the belief that the audience should only hear ideas, arguments and propositions, with the repetitions, clumsy formulations and hesitations removed. It was felt that an edited interview should have the mental throat-clearing removed so that the audience should get full informational value for its money. There were many occasions when the hesitant were made fluent, the verbose terse, the repetitious direct, the inordinately long remarkably concise, the dull almost interesting. (Television editing never aspired to this level of intervention. Yet it too offered the audience a sanitised version of the actual exchange in the studio.) Many politicians "lost" their first answer – in which they usually repeated what was already common ground between them, the interviewer and the audience – and gained the advantage of sounding exceptionally forthright in talking about the issue in question. (I always thought politicians' complaints about radio editing odd; most were hugely improved by the exercise.)

Yet the more it went on, the more did tidy editing and compact presentation become an obsession, an end in themselves: almost unbearably tidy and ultimately bossy in their outlook. A lot was lost, and much of it – in radio and television – went beyond the customary and inevitable need to sub-edit on grounds of space and time. There was a horror of any pauses. On one occasion, a senior editor, discussing a live extension to the previous evening's current affairs programme with the producer, was told that the transatlantic discussion had been a bit sticky. "Oh" he said, alarmed, "nobody stopped talking, did they?" That was the danger of going live. Then there was the equally undesirable characteristic of repetition. I sometimes wondered if we were all victims of the English public school system where the worst intellectual crime was to write an essay with a repetitious argument. It had to flow from the basic propositions of the opening paragraph to the well based conclusions of the closing one. So too went the Platonic ideal of the broadcast interview: a civilised exchange between intellectual partners, sharing similar assumptions, mutually conversant with each other's knowledge and dedicated to a genuine ideal, that of informing the audience. Repetition had no place in such a scheme of things. It was not an ignoble ideal, but it became increasingly irrelevant.

The arrival of the new breed of semi-official, Soviet spokesmen – journalists such as Alexander Bovin, broadcasters such as Vladimir Posner, academics such as Georgy Arbatov – shattered this cosy world. Any interview with them in the days of Brezhnevian stagnation when the party line was plausibly and staunchly defended – the more effectively in proportion to the excellence of the apologist's English – became a (usually pre-recorded) brawl. Given their ability to defend the indefensible and their dialectical skill, any interview ended up being five to ten minutes long. But the radio programme editor usually only had room for five. More to the point, they did not much like the brawl; it was untidy, it was repetitious, it did not tell the audience anything, it was not informative. But – it was said – once the disruptions and repetitions were removed, then it would "come down" to a neat five minutes. And so it usually did – telling the audience less than it should have done about the society and politics the spokesmen were defending. A form of interview posited entirely on the shared assumptions of a liberal democracy totally failed to adapt to the nasty business of confronting an autocratic totalitarianism.

In television the pattern was similar. In the beginning everything was live. The first tv mobile OB unit came into operation on May 2, 1937. Ten days later, it made history with the coverage (outside Westminster Abbey only) of the Coronation of King George VI. By 1945, internal BBC memos were considering the question of tele-recording, but seemed daunted by the difficulties and by the fact that film was so good. One memo suggested a camera combining a tv and film camera, with the film part automatically switched on when the tv camera was working. "One operator might manage the lot", suggested a somewhat despairing memo. Yet progress was being made. On Remembrance Day, 1947, television history was made when the Cenotaph Ceremony was transmitted live in the morning, special equipment filmed it off the screen at Alexandra Palace, and it was repeated in the evening. It had taken Philip Dorte and the BBC Television Film Unit a year to develop what a BBC official called, perhaps a bit patronisingly, a "temporary" system with "limitations".

More sympathetically, Philip Dorte told the *Daily Mail*: "Everyone who works at Broadcasting House is a television maniac and should be qualified for inclusion in Colney Hatch. Television engineers are notoriously wrapped up in their work, and all our wives are television widows".

Higher up in the BBC, Norman Collins, Head of Television Services in 1948, stated that the highest engineering priority was the development of television recording. America led the way: CBS first used videotape on tv on November 30, 1956, and it followed in Britain in 1958. The classic age of tv with its heavy use of video recording had arrived, and the production habits associated with it appeared to be both to be eternal and right.

Today, technology has once again set the broadcasters a fresh set of challenges – the fly-away satellite dish which allows live television reporting from anywhere in the world, and the growing availability of satellite channels or cable systems providing apparently unlimited space for non-stop reporting from wherever the single most important story is deemed to be coming. Who and how one story is deemed to merit such non-stop coverage is another matter. ISDN circuits offer radio the prospect of cheaper broadcasting at a far lower price from distant parts of the world. Broadcasting has changed from existing in a space and time limited environment to one where frequency space is becoming abundant, time almost unlimited, and money the only restraint.

This does not apply to every network in radio and television; but because it applies to some, or to an increasing number of them, it raises questions for all. You cannot build programmes to fill this amount of air time. The space will have to be filled with live broadcasting to a greater rather than a lesser extent. What kind of live will it be?

The answers to these questions rotate around a series of choices about the way that we want information to be provided. They relate to the balance between the instant and the considered; the topical versus the fundamental; the immediate rather than the analytical; the inclusive rather than the limited; the overall rather than the partial; the picture with more perspective rather than one with less. A live radio or tv news network will be radically different depending on the way that it strikes its own balance between these co-ordinates.

My own impulse as a broadcaster and my own interests as a listener turn towards a live, rolling radio news channel which is broad in its area of subject interest; which extends the news agenda, rather than limits it; which sets events in their place in the past rather than speculates on the place they may hold in the future; which offers reasons instead of guesses; rolling news should not be rolling repetition. This form of what I would call "Analysis News" would be subject to the same standards of news judgement as exist at present – they involve checking of sources, confirmation by others of initial reports, and no reduction of existing news editorial standards. They would not reduce live news – as occurred on occasion during the Gulf Crisis – to a "rip and read" service.

There is no point in setting up a huge news gathering, analysing and processing organisation if the standards under which it is alone worth doing are abandoned at the first twitch of an agency teleprinter. If you do not invest in news gathering and news processing, you should not pretend that you are offering a news service which arouses expectations of what such a service should provide. The danger of some versions of rolling news is that they give the impression that they place being first (and sometimes wrong) well ahead of being right and (occasionally) second. Critics and academics too must find a better yardstick of perform-ance measurement than which network was first with a particular story. To concentrate on this alone is to reduce information to the status of a horse race and does no service to the audience or the quality of the journalism.

The justification for the kind of News Analysis Channel that I have defined is that it is inclusive, comprehensive, treats subject matter, subjects and the audience with the respect that they deserve. Its richness of terms of reference allow it to vary the format as the news itself varies. The great pretence of journalists is that all the news is of the same weight each day, that the world is in an identical atmosphere of crisis every day, that every headline story is worth as much as the previous day's headline story. Of course, every television bulletin has to have a first story, every radio current affairs programme a lead subject, but journalists should admit to the audience more candidly than they do at present that we know the difference between a slow news day and a crisis, between a weak lead and a must lead, between a need to know and a nice to tell. A broadly based News Analysis Channel would have the intellectual grounding on which to base a more varied, more honest, more participatory agenda for the conveyance of news and information.

I do not in any sense rule out two other possible kinds of news channel, which I call Digest News and Events News. Digest News has its place and its utility and undoubtedly meets a demand. But its limitations should be recognised and acknowledged. The agenda is deliberately limited, the format repeated if not repetitious, the priority is given to concision and homogeneity. It tends to be premasticated to the point of tastelessness. Events News, the ability to follow one particular event to the exclusion of all others, also meets a need and as we saw with CNN during the Gulf War, can be extremely effective. Few would quarrel with such single issue treatment during world events such as the Gulf or the attempted coup against Gorbachev.

Of course, it is open to both a Digest News Channel and and Analysis Channel to choose to become an Events Channel for a particular time, a particular event and a specific duration. The question is: what event, and for how long? It may be right that we should have a dedicated Events Channel which only follows a single news event – those that I have already mentioned, or the William Kennedy Smith alleged rape trial, or the Clarence Thomas confirmation hearings for the supreme court.

Yet the danger with such coverage is that the question directed to all journalists all the time – "how do you decide what to include? How do you decide what to exclude?" – becomes virtually unanswerable in determining which tiny handful of events deserve covering on an Events Channel, or indeed on any other. How many watched the Clarence Thomas confirmation hearings because they were keen to see that a judge with appropriate legal qualifications was to be appointed to the highest court of the United States? Was the Kennedy Smith trial watched only because of an interest in justice and fair treatment of rape victims, rather than because they saw and heard things in that court room which they would never have been exposed to in the raunchiest tv detective series?

In covering events, live, continuously and to the the exclusion of all other, we need to have a very sensitive humbug detector. How does the public know that it wants to know only about event "A" when it is not told what other events it might also be interested in if it had the information. If ever journalists have to answer valid questions about their roles as gatekeepers to the news, then they must do so when they play this role in exhaustive coverage of specific events.

In a world of many networks and channels, the demand for any more news formats to fill them all may not be capable of satisfaction. Besides, there may be too many news channels even for the appetites of "Time Limited" listeners. With broadcasting space threatening to be so plentiful, we need new ideas to meet different kinds of audience interest. As any listener to the American radio broadcast scene knows, the one unifying ingredient is music; find your music niche and occupy it as thoroughly as possible, reassuring your specialist audience that the station will not risk positioning its programmes outside the strictly defined marketing niche. This works so far as it goes, but it does not go – is not intended to go – very far.

I believe we have not worked enough on the future possibilities of verbal streams of broadcasting, apart from news. If the time exists on frequencies waiting to be filled, what human interests might not be addressed and even satisfied if we looked for ways of communicating which do not rely almost exclusively on music? If the assumption is that some of the broadcasters and some listeners are "Time Unlimited" in their approach, and want something beyond niche music-radio, various thoughts occur as to new ways of filling the time. You could dedicate a speech network to, for instance, the practice of story telling, to the preservation of what remains of the oral tradition of western European culture, and even perhaps to its re-creation. The oral tradition could never have flourished in the Time Limited environment of broadcasting as it has existed or as its audience usually demands it. But long form radio – intimate, personal, ear to ear, intense, atmospheric, suggestive – belongs to an oral tradition to which it has never done justice. In 1902, R A Fessenden of the University of Pittsburgh first used radio waves to broadcast the human voice. Could it be that radio needs to rediscover its original impulse – the human voice talking?

Another network could be devoted to reading drama and poetry. I am not shocked by the thought that most people would not listen to the whole of "Hamlet" once a reading began. Most people have never listened to "Hamlet" in part or in whole under any circumstances. If anybody tuned in to a mere five minutes of a Shakespeare play, or Goethe, or the Bhagavad Gita, or a poem by Pushkin, would they be worse off than if they had never done so or would the work in question be diminished? Does making the written masterpieces of world literature available in this way diminish them or render them available and accessible, reintegrated into national culture in a way they have not been for years? I am a great believer in coming to terms with demanding art through accident, by hearing fragments, and so coming to terms with it as a whole. Having grown up in a "Time Limited" environment for the industry so far, I wonder if we are incapable of responding to the cornucopia of channels and networks now on offer because we do not realise that we have moved from "Time Limitation" to "Time Unlimitation" and that there is an audience waiting to be discovered for the latter too. It is almost certain that these new channels will be made up of live broadcasting because it is the cheapest way of filling the available air time.

As with most propositions, there is no need to sign up to it to the exclusion of others. The age of recording is not dead. It will still be a vital ingredient in the composition of live networks, and it will remain the essential tool for capturing some kinds of personal or political testimony which the live encounter in the studio will never be able to yield. Engagement in the studio; reflection in the recording; the appropriate technical forms for the appropriate means of expression; the choice of prose or poetry, a warm exchange or a cool one, the test of character or the judgement of experience.

Broadcasters have in their hands a more complete panoply of instruments of expression than they have ever had before, more technical facililty to blend the immediate, the reflected, the dramatic. Increasingly it will be governed by the wish and the possibility to present it in a context of live broadcasting. The best networks will be those which blend these heady ingredients most creatively. I rather think that Reith would have loved it.

First delivered to the Manchester University Broadcasting Symposium on 8 April 1992